The Soul Loves the Truth

Also by Denise Linn

Books
Altars
Dream Lover
*Feng Shui for the Soul**
The Hidden Power of Dreams
*If I Can Forgive, So Can You**
Past Lives, Present Dreams
Quest
Sacred Legacies
Sacred Space
The Secret Language of Signs
*Secrets & Mysteries**
Space Clearing
*Space Clearing A–Z**
*Soul Coaching**

Audio Programs
*Angels! Angels! Angels!**
Cellular Regeneration
*Complete Relaxation**
Dreams
*Journeys into Past Lives**
*Life Force**
Past Lives and Beyond
*Phoenix Rising**
The Way of the Drum

Videocassette
*Instinctive Feng Shui for Creating Sacred Space**

*Available from Hay House

Please visit Hay House USA: www.hayhouse.com®
Hay House Australia: www.hayhouse.com.au
Hay House UK: www.hayhouse.co.uk
Hay House South Africa: orders@psdprom.co.za
Hay House India: www.hayhouseindia.co.in

The Soul Loves the Truth

LESSONS LEARNED ON MY PATH TO JOY

DENISE LINN

HAY HOUSE, INC.
Carlsbad, California
London • Sydney • Johannesburg
Vancouver • Hong Kong • Mumbai

Published and distributed in the United States by: Hay House, Inc.: www.hayhouse. com • *Published and distributed in Australia by:* Hay House Australia Pty. Ltd.: www.hayhouse.com.au • *Published and distributed in the United Kingdom by:* Hay House UK, Ltd.: www.hayhouse.co.uk • *Published and distributed in the Republic of South Africa by:* Hay House SA (Pty), Ltd.: orders@psdprom.co.za • *Distributed in Canada by:* Raincoast: www.raincoast.com • *Published in India by:* Hay House Publications (India) Pvt. Ltd.: www.hayhouseindia.co.in • *Distributed in India by:* Media Star: booksdivision@mediastar.co.in

Editorial supervision: Jill Kramer • *Design:* Tricia Breidenthal

Library of Congress Cataloging-in-Publication Data

Linn, Denise.
  The soul loves the truth : lessons learned on my path to joy / Denise Linn.
     p. cm.
  ISBN-13: 978-1-4019-0746-4 (tradepaper)
  ISBN-10: 1-4019-0746-6 (tradepaper)
  1. Spiritual life. I. Title.
  BL624.L5445 2006
  204.092--dc22

                                                    2005035168

                        ISBN 13: 978-1-4019-0746-4
                        ISBN 10: 1-4019-0746-6

                 09 08 07 06   4 3 2 1
                      1st printing, June 2006

                 Printed in the United States of America

For my daughter, Meadow; and my husband, David;
I am so blessed to have you both in my life.

Contents

─∾∾•∾∾─

Preface

─∾∾•∾∾─

Reaching the Light

On August 5, 1967, I died from a gunshot wound. Well, that's what the doctors told me—they said that I "died" for a short time before I was resuscitated. Although the experience that landed me in the hospital was terrifying, as a result of it I learned one of my life's greatest lessons.

That day had started out great—everything seemed to be going my way. I was a 17-year-old teenager out for a carefree ride on my motorbike on a glorious, sunny afternoon. As I rode past tall cornfields in the countryside of my small farming community in Ohio, I had no idea that something would happen that would change my life forever. I didn't know that a man was following me and had been stalking me ever since he'd seen me on my motorbike earlier in the day. He didn't know me or anything about me; I was just in the wrong place at the wrong time.

For miles he slunk along in his car behind me, waiting until we were in an isolated area away from any farmhouses. Then, on a lonely stretch of the country road—and with a viciousness that was shocking to our sleepy Midwestern community—he rammed his car into the back of my motorbike. My spleen was instantly shattered from the impact of flying over the handlebars and skidding across the asphalt into a shallow ditch. As I struggled to get up, my attacker pulled his car up next to me. I hoped that he was going to help me, but a wave of disbelief pulsed through me when

I saw the steely hard look in his eyes . . . and then spied a gun in his hand. *A gun!* I couldn't believe what was happening to me.

When he squeezed the trigger, the air around me exploded like the force of steam bursting out of an engine. I crumpled back to the ground as the bullet ripped through me. The gravel felt sharp against my cheek. My eyes were closed, but I was still conscious as I heard him slam his car door and walk in my direction. As he hovered over me, I could hear his heavy breathing. Everything seemed to be going in slow motion and all sounds were amplified. I heard him unzipping something, followed by the sound of his gun being cocked again. I snapped open my eyes and looked up to find a young man with a sallow complexion and an oily smirk aiming his gun at me . . . again!

It's been said that life should be a joyous adventure and that we ought to head to the grave with wine in one hand and chocolate in the other, shouting, "Wow, what a life!" Unfortunately, that hasn't been the case for me. Sometimes I've felt as though I've been dragged along with a chain wrapped around one hand and a rope cinched to the other. My motto must have been "No pain, no gain" because my greatest lessons have come with much anguish and effort. It seemed that Spirit didn't care how scraped and bruised I got as long as I was learning and growing. I've experienced a lot of growth throughout the years, but almost everything came the hard way—especially what happened on that August day in 1967.

However, after many years of struggling through life, I've finally learned the secret: *We don't need to suffer to grow!* I wish that I'd learned it sooner, but now I do know that you *can* have wine in one hand and chocolate in the other as you sail into your future. You *can* live every moment with joy, no matter what's happening around you—it's often simply a matter of telling the truth to yourself!

In this book are some of the stories from my life that have propelled me to this realization. But the incident I suffered at age 17 perhaps tested me more than any other. That experience, in many ways, put me on the path that I now follow. Nevertheless, the valuable lessons I learned from this event on my path to joy definitely didn't come easily.

⁓

As I lay on the ground in excruciating pain with a gun pointed at me for the second time, so many questions raced through my head: *How did I end up in this situation? Why is this stranger trying to kill me? What did I do to him?* To this day, I don't understand what happened next. I was lying on the ground, helpless at the feet of a troubled man who'd plowed into me with his car, then shot me point-blank . . . and was about to fire at me again. Yet, remarkably, a sense of composure washed over me like a wave softly flowing onto the shore.

For some mysterious reason, all I felt for that unknown assailant at that moment was compassion—I could actually *feel* his pain and turmoil. Unfortunately, I could also feel his yearning to shoot me again. His actions were like that of an alcoholic who craves just one more drink, even though he knows he shouldn't. I could sense the internal struggle within him.

He fervently wanted to discharge his weapon into me, yet as I continued to look calmly into his eyes, he just couldn't pull the trigger. With a look of surprise, he turned his attention to the gun in his hand, which had begun to tremble. It was almost as if his hand had a mind of its own. Then his arm dropped limply to his side as he turned abruptly, quickly retreated to his car, and sped off.

Luckily, a man on his way home from work noticed me on the side of the road and stopped to investigate. Terrified by the sight of the blood, he frantically flagged down the next car and begged them to race into town to call the ambulance.

At the hospital, I was aware of people frantically shouting, "Someone's been shot! A girl's been shot!" Then suddenly all the pain disappeared, all the frightened voices faded away, and I found myself out of my body and surrounded by darkness. It was as though I were momentarily inside a large black sphere, which then burst open to reveal a land of golden light. It was majestic, tangible, radiant . . . and so familiar. *How could I have forgotten?* I thought as

I looked around at the luminescent landscape surrounding me. *It's my home . . . my true home! It's so good to be back.* (It was during this time that the doctors were certain I had died.)

Glorious music surrounded and swirled through me. Every cell in my being seemed to harmonize and vibrate with each note until I melted into the sweet rhythm. It sounds strange, even as I write this now, but I was no longer limited to my body. Instead, I was everywhere, merged with the golden light and the music . . . limitless and forever, without boundaries. At the same time, all beings—everyone who was in a physical body and everyone who had died—were also there, equally limitless. Somehow we were individuals, yet all one. I can't explain it, but it's what I experienced. And it all seemed normal. We weren't just part of each other, we *were* each other—we were literally the same being, yet separate and unique at the same time.

Merging with this infinite unity of all beings was love. In fact, there wasn't anything in the Universe that wasn't made up of love. *Everything was love*—it was the source of all that existed. I knew that I'd touched the heart of God. All were one, and all were love . . . and it seemed so natural. It was a different kind of love than I'd experienced on Earth, which always had an object; on Earth I loved something or someone, yet always felt a separation between that which I loved and myself.

The kind of love beyond death's door was universal and forever, without boundaries. In that heavenly place, there was no object for love. Love just was. I deeply regret that my words can't do justice to what I experienced. I saw that there was no evil in any soul . . . only beauty and grace. Although people do terrible things—as did the man who shot me—every cruel and thoughtless act was born out of fear, ignorance, or a sense of lack. I knew that feeling separate from this universal love was what caused people to do desperate and terrible things. I saw that all of creation was filled with Divine light and hallowed music. Everything was alive with Spirit—every atom, stone, blade of grass, tree, animal, mountain, and star. The Creator was everywhere and always. I was shown that there was no death—just change—and that we're each infinite and eternal.

As the golden light shimmered around me, I became aware that time had disappeared. There was no future or past . . . everything was a part of a flowing, infinite *now*. I tried to think of the past and I couldn't—it just didn't exist. I saw the futility of rehashing the past and how useless it was to worry about the future—for the past and future didn't actually exist. The only thing real was *now*. (I currently can't conceive of a reality with no time because I'm anchored into the time/space continuum of life in our world; however, I remember how profound it was at that moment to know that linear time, as I'd known it on Earth, absolutely did not exist.)

Flowing through this shimmering, vibrant Universe was a golden river of light. Across the river, I could see a far shore. The cord connecting me to my body was thin, and I knew that if I could reach the opposite shore, then this connection to my body would be severed and I could merge with the Source. I was so happy to release my attachment to the worldly plane.

When I stepped into the river, the liquid light flowed around me. Halfway across, I felt a "rope" tug hard at my midsection, and I felt as if I'd been lassoed. A deep and compassionate voice descended to tell me that my time on the planet wasn't complete—I had to return because I still had some things to do on Earth. But I didn't want to leave; I wanted to stay forever. I remember kicking and screaming in urgent protest as I grabbed at the cord around my waist, but in a flash I was yanked back into my body.

Back at the hospital, I was fighting for my life. I'd lost my spleen and adrenal gland, I had ruptures in my stomach, and my small intestines and left lung were severely damaged. I also had a bullet hole through my spine. (Eventually, I lost a kidney and had a six-inch tube inserted into my heart to replace the aorta.) In spite of the severity of my injuries, my body healed quickly. Doctors kept telling me that I was a miracle, and no one could believe that I was alive. But *I* knew that I'd been allowed to survive for a reason.

Even when we lose in life, it's important not to lose the lesson, and I learned so much the day I "died." My perception of life was totally altered by what had occurred: Before I was shot, life seemed to be a succession of meaningless events strung together in an uneven jigsaw puzzle that eventually led to death. But after my near-death experience, I saw life as a spiritual journey. I was shown that *all* the events of existence, even the traumatic ones, were essential for spiritual evolution. Compassion sprang forth from my heart when I saw that all human beings, even those who were cruel or selfish, were majestic and magnificent at their core. Each was an essential part of the great wonderment of life.

It would take years to comprehend and assimilate what I learned on the other side of death. But there were some things that I just "knew" immediately afterward. I absolutely knew, for example, that it was a blessing to be here on this planet, even in the bad times, and that there was a Divine plan for each of us. I understood that everything was good—*everything*—and eventually each occurrence in life would allow us to raise our level of consciousness.

Even though I was filled with these new revelations about the nature of life, in the weeks after I was shot, it was as if I had one foot in the world of the living and the other in the world of Spirit. On the one hand, I knew that nothing was bad—not even atom bombs, auto accidents, or miscarriages—because everything was absolutely a perfect part of God's Divine creation. And on the other hand, I had terrifying dreams of the man who tried to kill me. I was holding two deeply separate and opposing beliefs about the Universe: In one, the world was well ordered by Divine principles; while in the other, there was no order to the Universe at all—only a human struggle for survival amid fear and chaos.

At the same time that this dual awareness of reality was occurring, I was also deeply grieving the loss of my true home back in the land of golden light. I felt that it had all been ripped away from me when I was dragged back into my body. I'd gone from being connected to the Source to being exiled on Earth and feeling separate from love. The sense of loss was profound.

However, so much of the awareness that I gained on the Other Side lingered within me. I had discovered that invisible loving forces—guides, angels, and ancestors—gently guided our lives in accordance with our highest good. (Before I was shot, I would have called myself an atheist, since I'd adopted the belief system of both my parents, who were scientists.) I also learned that we don't have to die to bring the light of the Source into our lives—it's available for all of us, at all times. We don't need to deserve it; it's our spiritual heritage. It's simply a matter of believing and being open for it to flood into our lives.

Even as I struggled with severe pain while in the hospital, I felt extremely thankful for everything. As strange as it may sound, I was even grateful for being shot because I realized that it was a potentially positive event in my life. I think that I'd wandered so far off my path in life that it took an enormous wake-up call just to get me back on course. There's a well-known expression: "If you listen to the whispers, you don't have to hear the screams." In my case, the Universe had been whispering, and since I hadn't been open to hearing it, it finally screamed, "Denise, you're not what you think you are! I will show you the light, but it comes with a price!"

The "cosmic kick" that landed me in the hospital delivered the message directly and powerfully. From that point on, all the insights I gained on the Other Side began to penetrate and transform me. However, it wasn't always easy: Often along the way I'd forget who I was, and the truths that had been revealed to me on the Other Side would slip my mind. I'm ashamed to say that getting shot wasn't the only time in my life that I was forced to "hear the screams."

Even after having the wondrous insights revealed to me during my near-death experience (about how to live life with joy), over and over again I still found myself in challenging, difficult, or humiliating circumstances. Although I learned something from each experience and would even think, *Right, God—okay, I got it; I'll remember who I am now,* somewhere down the line I'd forget again. I'd neglect to search for the truth in my soul. I'd fail to remember that I'm lovable and beautiful. I'd overlook the fact that there is a sacred plan for us all. I wouldn't recall that we don't have to struggle and use so much effort to stay in the flow of our destiny. I'd stop believing that I was a part of all things . . . that I wasn't separate from the world around me. And I'd forget that I was safe and didn't need to put up protective barriers around myself.

I've learned so much in my life, but unfortunately, wisdom hasn't come easy for me. As a way of dealing with the events of my life, I often told myself that "Pain equaled gain" and "Suffering built character"—beliefs that seemed to make sense since my life was so full of pain and suffering. Over time, however, the lessons learned from my "death" did filter their way deep into my very being and take root in my soul . . . and some of these lessons have made their way into this book. I now know that we don't need to suffer to grow, and no matter what our pasts have been, we *can* sail into the future with a glass of wine in one hand and chocolate in the other while shouting with glee! ⊙∰~

Introduction

The Soul Loves the Truth

*A*s I've mentioned, I've gone through a lot in my life, and not all of it was positive. In fact, some of it was downright horrific and frightening . . . yet I've come out on the other side. Although there were many years when I was sure I'd never experience happiness or joy, I now wake up in the morning filled with delight.

This book contains some of the stories from my life and the lessons that I learned from those experiences. Each of these events has propelled me on my path to inner peace and has permitted me to understand the world in a way that finally makes sense. These life experiences have allowed me to comprehend the profound reality that *the soul loves the truth.*

Perhaps you've heard the expression "The truth will set you free." This is a spiritually potent statement, because when you do tell the truth to yourself—without embellishing anything and without apology or guilt—you're free. It's the kind of freedom that allows you to be present in the moment, without rehashing the past or worrying about the future. It allows you to relinquish the burden of fulfilling the needs of others, while denying your own. And it's the liberty to clearly hear the sacred voice of your soul without the interference of your preconceived beliefs and habitual thought patterns.

My journey to joy started with telling myself the truth about the circumstances of my life . . . and this was often incredibly difficult.

It was grueling to shine the bare light of truth on dark and hidden parts of my past, and some of the stories in this book are about just that: facing the truth of the past, without excuses or shame. And I share how you can do this, too, in order to gain benefits for your life. Other stories included herein are about understanding that the challenging circumstances of life always come with a lesson, and it's through experience that we grow.

All of the stories in this book come from my life, and every one is meant to stand on its own, so it's not necessary to read them in any particular order. My intent is that the right story will appear to you at just the right time in your life. Some recount the pain I've gone through (and the lessons I've learned as a result), while others contain my observations about the world around me—but every one contains insights culled from my experiences. (Several of these stories have appeared in my other books, but they're included here because many people have expressed their gratitude for the value that they gained from them . . . so I beg your forgiveness if you've read them before.)

After each account, there's a section called "Steps to Empowerment," which you may find helpful. By doing some of these exercises, you might just discover that your odyssey to self-awareness becomes easier and more fruitful.

It is my sincerest desire that you'll find bliss in your life easily and effortlessly simply by reaching into your soul and honoring the truth that resides there. Thank you so much for joining me on this journey.

CHAPTER ONE

Take Risks, but Look Before You Leap

Once You're Committed, Keep Going

I was a 19-year-old college student at Michigan State University when I decided that I wanted to learn to skydive. I loved the idea of gently floating through the air while peacefully looking down at the world below. However, my lofty idea was very different from the reality . . . as I was soon to learn.

When I discovered that the small airport near campus had a parachute club, I eagerly signed up for instruction. As the early-morning class began, the beefy, ruddy-faced instructor explained to our small group how to roll up an open parachute to ready it for a jump. He then had us line up and, one at a time, climb on the old barrel that was next to the hangar and practice a technique for landing after a jump. We had to leap off the wobbling barrel, keep our ankles together, and then do a fast-paced tuck and roll onto the ground. That was it—that was the entire class. We were then told that we were ready to skydive.

"Well, let's go!" the instructor directed.

"We're ready?" I inquired, unable to hide the doubt in my voice. I thought, *There has to be more training. After all, we're going to jump out of an airplane. Don't we need more instruction?*

"Hurry up—we'll help you get your suits on," he declared, without regard for my concern. So, after our chutes were strapped to our backs, we all walked toward a small twin-engine plane.

"See that guy?" the instructor asked, pointing to the side of the runway where a man in a wheelchair looked on mutely. "He lost both of his legs on a jump here, but he still comes back to watch." He stated this as if it were a badge of honor.

As I waited to board the plane, I looked back over my shoulder at the man in the wheelchair. He looked wistful, yet tired and sad. Nevertheless, I squeezed myself into the plane and waited for the pilot. A slightly moldy smell mixed with gasoline fumes filled the air. As I buckled myself in, the propellers started, and the plane shuddered as the engines revved. With a lurch we began to pick up speed as we raced down the bumpy runway. When we lifted up off the ground, my stomach leapt into my throat.

Soon we were flying high over the fields below. The sound of the engines roared in my ears and distracted me from what I was about to do. I glanced at the guy sitting next to me—it was also his first jump—his face was white and drawn. I was a little worried that he might throw up, so I subtly slid as far away from him as I could.

Our instructor, who now referred to himself as "the jump-master," was sitting, unafraid, next to the open door. He shouted at us over the noise of the plane: "In just a moment, you're going to stand out on the strut of the airplane. Remember to hold on with both hands!" He really didn't need to remind me of that—I was most certainly going to hold on with everything I had.

"While you're standing out there, I'm going to look out the door. When we fly over a good place for you to jump, I'll tap the side of your leg. Then just let go and have a good time!" he continued over the noise.

"Oh, and I almost forgot: You're not on a static line, so remember to pull your rip cord!"

The jumpmaster then pointed at me to go. My heart jolted. As I moved forward to stand in the open door, my shirt flapped wildly in the wind. *I can do this! I can do this!* I repeated to myself, hoping that it was true. The air whipped in my face with such force that I had trouble breathing.

Clutching the door, I willed my wobbly legs not to buckle beneath me, as I leaned out to carefully grab the bar on the underside of the wing, first with one hand and then with the other. Next, I stepped completely outside the plane and stood on the strut, holding on as tightly as I could. As I gazed below, everything appeared to be really tiny. Farmhouses gave the impression of being little wooden toys, while fields looked like a perfect patchwork of brown and green squares.

The jumpmaster leaned his head out and glanced up at me. Seemingly satisfied, he looked down to make sure it was a good place for me to jump, and then he slapped me hard on the side of my leg. This was my signal to go . . . but my hands just wouldn't let go. They were attached to the bar as if they had a will of their own.

Thinking that I'd missed my jump spot, I reached inside the open door to get back into the plane. The jumpmaster gave me a surprisingly brutal look and wrenched my hand off the door.

"What are you doing?" I screamed, grabbing the door again with my right hand. He lurched forward, gripped his large hand around my wrist, and yanked at my left hand while I squirmed to hold on to the bar. I felt as if I were in a life-or-death struggle. As I frantically tried to get back into the plane, he kept pushing me out.

Oh my God—has he gone mad? He's trying to force me out of the plane. He's going to kill me! I thought, panic-stricken, as I looked at the long drop to the earth below.

Finally, with immense effort, the jumpmaster pried both my hands free and threw me out. While I was falling, I continued to claw at the air as if it were still possible to get back into the plane. I desperately thought, *I have to get back in there!* As I fell farther and farther away, the instructor waved at me with a big smile. A fierce hatred surged through me at that moment, but then I looked down . . . and saw that the ground was getting close very quickly. I quit thinking about how to return to the safety of the plane, and realized that I had to do something—now, so I grabbed my rip cord and yanked on it as hard as I could.

Thankfully, my chute whipped open. It twirled me around in the air a few times before it slowed down my descent. Then I just floated gently, suspended in time. It was beautiful, serene, and amazingly quiet. I felt as if I might drift in the sky forever, although it probably was only a few seconds. Then the ground appeared to be rapidly approaching. Just in time, I remembered to put my ankles together. When I hit the bare field, it was with both feet. I tucked and rolled just as I'd learned in my ten-minute training. *I did it!* I was exuberant. I took a deep breath and expelled it powerfully, completely satisfied with my accomplishment.

After rolling up my chute, I walked toward the airstrip and waited for the plane to land.

"What were you trying to do up there, kill me?" I challenged the instructor as he deplaned.

"That's the funniest thing I've ever seen. You sure looked hilarious trying to swim back to the plane," he laughed. "Once you go out on the strut, we never let you back in. You should have known that. Your chute might have deployed and gotten caught in the propeller. I *had* to throw you out," he chuckled.

"Well, that would be a good thing to tell someone *before* they step out of the plane! No one ever told me that!" I yelled uselessly as he walked away, practically holding his sides with laughter.

Despite not feeling prepared for this experience, I soon found out that I'd actually been very successful. I was the only first-time jumper that day who hadn't been injured. I felt sorry when I learned that the guy with the pale face had broken his leg upon landing. The truth was that the safety standards taught in that instructor's class were considerably subpar. A month later, I heard that another first-time jumper died at that same airfield. This may have had something to do with my decision not to pursue skydiving as a hobby. Yet the experience *did* bring me several important lessons.

ONCE ON THE STRUT, NEVER GO BACK

One thing I found out that day was that when I make a commitment to take a risk, it's important for me to see it through . . . even if I'm scared or uncertain. Often in the last moments before I attempt something new—even if it's as mundane as learning a skill or adopting a different attitude about life—my mind will come up with a thousand reasons why it's not a good idea. Then I remember how the jumpmaster said that once you're out on the strut, you can never go back. To me this means that once I make a decision, I need to push past my fear, and immediately and decisively follow through with my plan. By hesitating when I was on that plane's strut, I potentially put myself—and everyone else on the plane—at risk. I'd already made the choice to jump, so my last-minute vacillation didn't serve me or anyone else.

Of course, prior to making a risky decision, it's a good idea to give yourself plenty of time to weigh the pros and cons of the plan, just as it's *not* a good idea to attempt something new without proper preparation. However, once you've done your homework and come to your final resolution, don't get sidetracked by last-minute fears and indecision. It's important to act quickly and with resolve. Make a commitment to yourself to step forward with passion and determination . . . and follow through without looking back. Second-guessing yourself or regretting a decision you've made is like trying to drive a car forward while looking in the rearview mirror—it won't help you get where you want to go.

When I plunged through the sky on my jump, I spent vital seconds looking back instead of attending to the present. I almost forgot to pull my rip cord because I was wasting time regretting my decision to parachute, being mad at the jumpmaster, and even futilely trying to get back in the plane. If I'd continued to hesitate by keeping my awareness on past events, rather than being present and noticing how soon I was going to hit the ground, I might have been another first-time casualty (as well as not being able to enjoy those precious moments of serenity).

STEPS TO EMPOWERMENT

Is there an area of your life in which you want to make a commitment or take a risk but have continually been afraid? It might be something as big as whether to accept a new job or to move to a new city, or something as small as a changing your hairstyle or making a purchase that's been on your mind. Although consciously you may agonize over what decision to make, deep inside you already know whether or not it's something you truly want to do. Listen to that voice, and trust that it will lead you in the right direction. Honesty nourishes the soul—once you've opened your heart to discover the answer and have carefully prepared and thought it through, you're ready to take that leap of faith. Then just do it . . . jump! Don't hesitate—do it with resolve. Once you get out on the strut of life, keep moving forward and don't turn back.

BELIEVE THAT
IT'S POSSIBLE!

While studying journalism at Michigan State, I was awarded a grant to attend an international journalism conference in the former Yugoslavia. Although I'd only been working at a small newspaper, this was an opportunity to meet journalists from major print publications around the world and to travel to a foreign seaside town in the Balkans. Reporters from *Time* magazine, *Izvestia* in Russia, and *The Observer* in the United Kingdom were expected to participate—and I imagined the riveting intellectual conversations we'd have as we sat around a table with a bottle of wine and talked late into the night.

Unfortunately, group dynamics being what they sometimes are, the social interactions of the conference didn't shape up the way I would have liked. This was mostly due to the presence of a capricious young woman named Trisha. She dominated the group from the start, and everyone followed her lead. Men in particular seemed to hang on her every word, as though whatever she said was infinitely more interesting than anything the group may have been discussing.

Trisha and I were complete opposites: Her blonde hair was effortlessly glamorous, while my brunette locks hung limply. She dressed as if she'd just stepped out of the pages of a fashion magazine, while I wore jeans and peasant shirts. She had slender, graceful fingers and carefully manicured nails, which glistened and shone like ripe cherries; and I had big utilitarian hands and short, stubby nails. She had the look of someone who was on her way to a country-club social function, while I looked like I was about to hitch a ride in the back of a pickup to a hippie commune.

Trisha disliked me almost immediately, and I really didn't care for her either. She went out of her way to taunt me in front of the others: In the syrupy tones of her phony Southern accent, she caustically judged my political beliefs—I was against the war in Vietnam, and she was for it—my appearance, and even my fingernails. "Denise, you should take those working-woman hands you've got there and get something done about those nails," she drawled. Oh, how she infuriated me!

One time, she remarked loudly to the group as I walked in, "My, my—will you look at what the cat has dragged in this time." She thought that she was funny and was doing a great service to the group by keeping them entertained at my expense. I could sense the animosity beneath her words and felt like an innocent victim of her mean-spiritedness. It didn't occur to me at the time that I was directing the same ill will toward her with my thoughts. The only difference between our attitudes was that I wasn't vocalizing mine to everyone within earshot.

I spent much of my time during the conference trying to figure out how I could get over my judgments about Trisha. Then one day I overheard her telling the group about how she'd climbed the cliffs by the ocean and discovered the most magnificent view from the top. I could hardly believe it! Trisha, the woman who was afraid to break a nail and complained that swimming in the ocean discolored her hair, had *climbed* to the top of those steep ragged bluffs at the ocean's edge.

How did she do it? Maybe she isn't the woman I think she is. Shaking my head in disbelief, I looked down at my own hands and marveled at their size and strength. *If she could climb those cliffs, surely I could do it, too.* I was a little skeptical at the prospect of climbing a towering cliff that plunged into the sea, but if Trisha had done it, then it must be possible. I made up my mind that I was going to do it, too.

The next morning I awoke at the break of dawn, determined to see the view from the top and make it back for the start of that day's conference. The face of the bluffs was somewhat visible from town, and it only took me about 40 minutes to walk there. From the rocks at the bottom, the cliffs rose nearly 300 feet high. The side

I planned to ascend appeared to have an almost 90-degree angle. This was long before rock climbing became a popular activity, and I knew nothing about the need for gear or the necessity of taking safety precautions. I visualized myself reaching the top, shook out my legs, and thought, *I have no idea how Trisha could have ever climbed this thing, but if she can do it, I know that I can.* And then, armed with that determination, I reached up with my hand, found a place to grab hold, and started my ascent.

It seemed as if the ability to climb was innately present within me, as I wedged my fingers and toes into little places to gain leverage before hoisting myself up in spurts. But little by little, my hands began to tingle, my forearms tightened and pulsated in pain, and the tips of my fingers began to be rubbed raw from the abrasive rock surface (in fact, some blood had started to ooze from one of them). I was gripping with all my might, but I feared that my muscles might give out and my hands might slip, and I'd be sent tumbling down the rock face. But whenever I felt like giving up, I pictured Trisha's shiny red nails and thought, *If she did this with those fingernails, I can definitely do it, too.*

I was able to get a little farther up before fear really started to take a hold of me. When I looked down at the waves crashing violently on the black rocks below me, I felt really frightened. I was so high above them by that point that I knew it would be a long fall if I didn't make it to the top. It was getting harder to find outcroppings to grab, and the crevices in which I could cram my feet were getting smaller and smaller. A few times I'd grasp an overhang, only to have the dirt around it break off and crumble in my hand, and I'd have to quickly find another projection to take hold of without letting go with my other hand. Yet I just kept visualizing myself reaching the top of the cliff.

On a slightly less-vertical section of the climb, I lost my footing momentarily and started to slide back down the rock. In a panic, I reached for anything I could find, and eventually got a hold of a tiny root sticking out of the cliff. I hung on to it as tightly as I could while regaining my footing. Every time I wanted to give up, I'd hear these words in my head: *If she can do it, so can I.*

Before long, the top of the cliff was in sight, and it actually seemed possible that I'd make it the last 30 feet. I was holding on to a tiny bulge in the rock with both hands, and my feet were firmly wedged in a couple of small holes, when I realized that I'd come to an impasse. Reaching above me as far as my arm could stretch, I was unable to find any handhold. I was stuck there, resting my weight on my legs and alternating between the hand that held me up and the one that searched for the next support that would take me higher. The rock face felt smooth and seamless, and I feared that I might have reached the end of my journey and would have to go back down. But when I attempted to retrace my steps, I couldn't find anywhere to put my foot. It was impossible.

Suddenly, it occurred to me that it might be even harder to get back down the cliff. I was stuck—I couldn't go up, and I couldn't go down. I tried to stay calm while I considered what to do next. The sun was pounding on my back as it continued to rise higher in the sky. Sweat beaded up on my skin and made my palms slippery. My arms were shaking, my legs were exhausted, and my toes were cramping from the pressure. I looked below to see if anyone on the shore had taken notice of my predicament, but there was no one in sight. I was alone . . . I was scared . . . and my options had run out. It seemed that nothing short of a miracle would save me.

I hung there for what seemed like hours. Just as my body was about to give up, my eye caught sight of the tiniest bright blue flower growing out of a small opening above me. It was surviving in a precarious position, for it was teetering on the edge of the cliff and getting knocked around by ocean winds, but it was somehow managing to survive on the small amount of dirt found in the crack. It seemed that even that little amount of soil was enough to provide the flower with the nutrients it needed.

I considered the blossom's unique grace and beauty, as well as the way it used the cliff to exist, and a sense of peace filled my entire being. I knew that I was being shown this flower for a reason . . . and then I knew what to do.

I was no longer fighting against the cliff, I was connected to it—part of it. The cliff and I were no more separate than the cliff and the flower. We were one and the same. I was the tiny flower that had managed to survive on the sheer rock face, and I was the cliff. Feeling a calmness wash over me, I reminded myself that if Trisha could climb this cliff, I certainly would have no problem doing it. Over and over I told myself, *If she can do it, so can I.*

I stretched up as far as I could to place my fingertips where the crack in the rock was that held the flower. Amazingly, my fingers fit perfectly, and the fissure held my weight. I pulled myself up and easily found the next projection to grab. I felt as if the cliff were reaching out and handing me ledge after ledge so that I could climb up. Finally, with one last motion, I propelled myself up over the top edge, rolled onto the flat ground, and exhaled with immense relief.

As I lay there, I looked out at the ocean and realized that it had taken me the better part of a day to reach the top. The sun had dropped near the horizon and was shining its golden light on me as if to congratulate my achievement, and sparkles of light bounced beautifully and brightly across the water with the energy of a standing ovation. I jumped to my feet and raised my arms to the sky . . . I'd done it! And it felt even better than I had imagined! When I peered back over the edge, I could hardly believe that I'd climbed up the entire cliff. I smiled down at the little blue flower, even though I could no longer see the place where it grew. I wasn't sure how I was going to get back, but I felt a deep, relaxed certainty that I could do it.

Although I couldn't understand how Trisha had endured the climb, I felt strangely connected to her at that moment—she'd been right about the view! Then, as I backed away from the dangerous edge of the bluffs, I caught a glimpse of something out of the corner of my eye. I turned around and shrieked as I realized that there were not only the ruins of an old monastery behind me, but there was also a well-marked road leading back to town. I immediately realized that Trisha *had* climbed to the top of the cliff to see the view . . . only she hadn't arrived there as I had—she'd clearly used the road. As I looked back in the direction of the cliff, I realized how incredibly fortunate I was to have survived the climb, *and* how lucky I was that I could return via the road rather than climb back down the rock face!

It was late evening when I got back, and the conference had long since ended for the day. Part of me wanted to tell everyone what I'd done, but I had a sneaking suspicion that the story of my great climbing feat would only incur further ridicule for attempting something so dangerous. Instead, I just got in bed and lay there quietly, thinking about the serene little blue flower on the edge of the steep cliff.

The next day, there was a buzz in the small village about an amazing event that had occurred the day before. Everyone wanted to know who the mysterious woman was who'd climbed the ocean bluffs to the monastery. Apparently, it had never been done successfully before. The only other person who'd ever attempted it was a man from France . . . and it was said that he'd died from a fall during his climb.

Before long, word got out that of one the townspeople had used binoculars to take a closer look and had noticed that the climber was wearing a peasant shirt. It soon became clear to everyone that I was the local celebrity. From that point on, whenever I went into town, someone always bought me a drink and asked me to tell them about my climb. Sometimes I'd even stay out late into the evening, sitting around a table with a bottle of wine, and retelling my story about how I'd made it to the top of the cliff.

If You Believe That You Can . . . You Can

I think that the reason I was able to climb the cliff was because I absolutely believed that it was possible, even in the face of adversity. I was convinced that if Trisha, who was physically not as strong as I was, could scale a steep mountain, then I'd be able to do it, too. This certainty became the driving force that allowed me to push past the pain in my body and the very real fear of falling. In other words, believing that you *can* and *will* accomplish a task is the most powerful motivator you can have. It's what will enable you to overcome any doubt or fear that you may have.

Take, for example, the fact that for years it was believed to be impossible to run faster than a four-minute mile. Scientists said that the human body simply wasn't capable of going that fast; and some runners feared that if they did break through this perceived barrier, then they might permanently damage their bodies or even die. And then, against the odds, Roger Bannister did it in 1954, running the mile in 3:59.4. If you asked him, he probably would have told you that he believed he could do it, even before he shattered the record. What's more remarkable still is the fact that the following year, several other men also broke the four-minute-mile barrier. You might wonder how so many people were able to do it the next year, when no one had been successful during all prior years. I believe that the answer is simply that once they knew that it was possible, they believed *they* could do it, too—and consequently they could! Now running the four-minute mile is commonplace.

If there's something in your life that you desire, but you're afraid to attempt it or doubt that it's possible, the first steps are to *know* that it's possible and to believe in yourself. Question what's making you fearful, and be willing to step beyond it. You must believe with your whole heart that it *is* possible, and that you *can* accomplish it.

Successful people have a clear vision of what they desire, and even if they're afraid, they're certain that they can reach their goals. You see, even though having a vision is extremely important, it's not enough—you also need to *believe* that you can actually achieve your goal and then focus on ways to reinforce that belief. Visualize it happening, notice your fear, and don't hide from it—instead, use that fear to propel you toward your goal. Powered by your belief in yourself, push beyond your supposed limitations so that you'll be able to scale mountains and attain anything you put your mind to.

STEPS TO EMPOWERMENT

What goals have you been unable to reach because of fear? Make a list of every seemingly unattainable aim and write each one down on the left side of a piece of paper. Then list any fears or doubts you have that are related to it on the right side. Be sure to note every excuse that you've made for why this goal is beyond your reach. Being honest with yourself is the key to moving forward and realizing your intentions—remember, your soul loves the truth.

Once you have your list of goals and limiting factors, examine them in a thoughtful and authentic way, one at a time. For each fear or doubt, ask yourself if there's any way that you can come up with a phrase to push beyond it and get closer to your goal. For example, if you want to change professions but are afraid that you won't be able to pay the bills if you do, give yourself an affirming phrase to say, such as, *If I can make it in my current job, I can make it in my new one.* When I was climbing the cliff, I used the phrase *If she can do it, so can I* to help me make it to the top of the cliff. These kinds of verbal or mental affirmations can be immensely helpful toward achieving your goal.

Another step you can take is to imagine how your life would be if you had that new career. The key to doing so is to actually believe that it's possible. My belief that I *could* get to the top of the cliff, and then visualizing myself there, allowed me to make my climb. And always begin your endeavor by knowing that you can attain your dream: Visualize that your new job will not only pay your bills, for instance, but will also allow you to enjoy life's luxuries.

The next step is to take action. For example, if you want that new career, find ways to gradually change professions. Volunteer or work part-time in the new field while you keep your current job. In this manner, you'll gain experience in your new career, and your current income won't suffer. When you believe that it's possible and then take action, anything *is* possible.

The power of believing in yourself and in your ability to reach your goal can't be underestimated. If you continue to do this exercise over and over again, and you find ways to reinforce your belief in yourself, eventually your doubts and fears will no longer be barriers to your dreams. Trust in your strength and look for the little blue flowers along the way.

~⚬~

LISTEN
WITH YOUR
HEART

When I was in college, I learned that things aren't always what they seem. I discovered this truth while spending a semester in Hawaii, doing an independent study on the coverage of world events by an island newspaper. Even though my younger sister, Heather, lived in Honolulu and allowed me to stay with her, I had very little money. I needed to find a part-time job quickly, so I scanned the newspaper and eventually saw an ad for DANCE PARTNERS NEEDED. I envisioned a glamorous studio where Fred Astaire and Ginger Rogers twirled around on a well-polished ballroom floor.

Hey, this is great! I thought. *I love to dance, and I can get paid to do it, too!*

When I called, the man who answered the phone said that the studio was kind of like an Arthur Murray–type place, but I didn't need experience—and they'd even provide transportation! It sounded like the perfect job; in fact, when the driver came to pick me up in a long, shiny black car, I couldn't believe my good luck. For a few moments, I imagined that this might be how a rock star felt traveling to the next big performance.

Looking out the car window, however, I soon noticed that we'd entered a seedy part of town: Harsh blinking lights, peep shows, and high-heeled prostitutes lined the street. And the car pulled up in front of a building with neon lights that flashed, "Girls! Girls! Girls!"

Oh my God! I thought, feeling the color drain from my face. *What have I gotten myself into?*

"It's on the second floor. Just go up those stairs there," the driver said gruffly, pointing toward an outdoor staircase and motioning for me to get out. I hesitantly stepped out on the sidewalk, and the car sped away down the street.

Maybe it's a big studio that's located in this part of town for space purposes, I speculated rather hopefully. *Perhaps the flashing sign refers to the business next door.* As I walked up the wide, dimly lit stairs, I tried to ignore the large rat that scuttled out in front of me.

I don't know why I didn't bolt. I think I had a crazy idea that when I opened the door at the top of the stairs, I'd be in a brightly lit ballroom . . . and I'd have the great job I had imagined. However, when I reached the top of the stairs, the door opened and a small Asian man ushered me into a dark, smoke-filled room. It definitely wasn't the studio I'd imagined. I was introduced to the manager, an overweight, Caucasian man in his mid-40s, who'd waddled over to welcome me.

"It's an easy job, and it pays well," he said through puffs on his cigar. "When the music starts, a man will come up to you and ask you to dance. He'll have a row of tickets with him that he purchased for 50 cents each. He needs to give you one ticket for each dance. At the end of the night, you hand in your tickets, and we give you 25 cents per ticket. It's easy!"

Well, this sure wasn't what I had in mind, but I'm already here . . . it can't hurt to try it for just one night, I thought with deep disappointment. I had my heart set on a sparkling ballroom, not this shady place. But the job didn't sound too difficult, so I walked over to one side of the dance floor and sat in a row with all the other girls. Seeing the men sitting on the other side of the room, I was instantly reminded of a scene from one of my eighth-grade dances.

As I sat there looking around at the other girls, I realized that I didn't exactly fit in. All the other gals were Asian and much shorter than I was. They all wore sexy, low-cut dresses and layers of mascara, lipstick, and rouge. I was tall, dressed modestly (in comparison anyway), and my only makeup was a smudge of pale pink lipstick.

Through the haze of smoke, I tried to look at the men across the room. It was so dark that I couldn't really see their faces or the shapes of their bodies. All I *could* see was a row of crisply starched and ironed white shirts that glowed eerily in the black lights. As the guys shifted slightly in their seats, the shirts seemed to move on their own, like a row of disembodied spirits out of a scary movie. I found out later that the men who frequented these clubs were typically from the Philippines. They worked in Hawaii and sent money back home to their families.

As a new song started to play, a fellow shyly approached me with his hand outstretched, offering me a ticket. All the other girls tucked the tickets seductively into their bras, but I wasn't sure what to do with the one the man had given me. I didn't want to stick it in my bra, so I just clutched it tightly in my hand. It was a slow song—I soon realized that *all* the songs were slow—and we were an awkward pair. He was very short, compared to my height of 5'8". His head was level with my chest . . . in fact, it kind of disappeared between my breasts, and he snuggled into them quite contentedly.

About a minute into the dance, the music stopped. Furtively, he handed me another ticket as the music began again. Every time the music stopped, he handed me another ticket, and I was soon clutching a handful of tickets. In this fashion, my one dance actually earned me a large number of tickets. With each new dance partner, however, I began to feel more and more uncomfortable. This certainly wasn't Fred Astaire I was dancing with, and I definitely wasn't Ginger Rogers . . . so I knew that it was time to look for another job. I left without cashing in my tickets and hailed a cab. I was just happy to be out of that situation as I headed safely back to my sister's apartment.

The next morning, Heather chided me: "Denise, you are so gullible! How do you always get yourself into these situations?" It was embarrassing to be taken to task by my younger sister. However, this wasn't the first time in my life that I'd been asked that question. In fact, I'd heard this same sentiment expressed many times by many different people as I wandered into, and luckily out of, some pretty strange experiences.

Don't Just Open Up Your Ears . . .

In my life, I've gotten into a lot of sticky—and even har-rowing—situations because of my naïveté. Although I absolutely believe that it's important to see the best in people and to take others at their word, I also believe that it's important to be discern-ing. If I'd listened carefully with my intuition, as well as with my ears, I would have realized that the man who answered the phone concerning the dance-partner job wasn't telling me the whole truth about the situation.

There have been many other times in my life when I could have been spared a lot of heartache if only I'd listened with my heart as well as my head. One of the saddest examples of this happened while I was a student at Michigan State. If only I would have known how to listen with my heart, I could have escaped an immense amount of suffering.

During my time in college, I lived with my boyfriend, Ron, in a small farmhouse that we shared with another couple on the out-skirts of town. At one point in our relationship, something didn't feel right, so I asked Ron if he was having an affair. When he denied it, his eyes shifted back and forth, his breathing became a bit more rapid, and his muscles tensed. I wanted so much to believe him, so I accepted what my ears heard him say. I chose not to acknowledge what my heart was hearing—that he *was* cheating on me with one of my friends.

I denied the truth for so long that when a mutual friend finally told me about the affair, I landed in the hospital because of a sui-cide attempt. *How could he have lied to me?* I bemoaned. But the truth was that although he'd lied with his words, his body language and energy had screamed out, *I'm having an affair, Denise!* But I didn't want to believe it, so I put on blinders. I could have avoided the emotional anguish, the medical expenses, and the humiliation of an attempted suicide if only I'd been willing to listen with my heart and move on to a better situation.

I've since learned then that when people aren't telling the truth, their words and actions often give them away. For example, if I ask a salesperson, "Is this a good product?" and he hesitates or looks off to one side instead of looking at me straight in the eyes when he says "Yes," then he's probably not telling the truth. Or if he answers in a halted manner, "Um, oh yeah, this is, um, a great product," he probably doesn't believe in what he's selling.

I used to take everyone at face value, but now I've learned that words are a very small part of true communication. To perceive the accuracy of what's being said, it's important to feel the energy beneath the spoken words, as well as to watch the body language of the person. Even if people look you in the eye and don't hesitate in their communications but you feel unsure or hesitant about what they're saying, then there's a chance that something more is going on beneath their words.

Sometimes individuals give out all the signals that say, "Don't trust me" (such as shifting eyes and halting language), but we're so attached to a desired outcome that we miss the truth about what's actually happening. For example, I was so attached to the idea that I could work at an Arthur Murray–type studio *and* that my boyfriend was faithful that I didn't allow myself to hear the whole truth about either situation.

STEPS TO EMPOWERMENT

Examine all aspects of your life, including your relationships, career, creativity, sexuality, and spirituality—is there an area in which you're listening with your ears instead of your heart? Deep inside you, there's a place that does know the truth. Trust your intuition, and let it be your guide. You have the power to know if you're being lied to or not. You also have the ability to know if you're lying *to yourself* or not.

There are some techniques that can help you discover these truths if you're unable to hear your intuition in your everyday life, or when you find yourself encountering situations or people who demand that you ignore the messages from your heart.

First, find a calm, quiet place to relax, and enter into a meditative state. Once you're there, visualize yourself in a beautiful location in nature that feels comfortable and safe to you. Ask yourself what the truth is about a particular situation or person and listen for your answer. You can also envision yourself talking to a wise being or sage and asking him or her to reveal the answers to your questions. Often one of these methods is enough to unlock your intuition.

Another thing that might help is to imagine a set of three lights in front of you: one red, one green, and one yellow. As you ask each question, notice which light brightens in your mind. The red light signifies that the answer to your question is no, while the green light means that the answer is yes. The yellow light may mean that there isn't enough information to make a decision, so when you see it, you should attempt to gather more information about the situation or person, and proceed with caution until you can come to a better understanding about the truth.

These methods can be powerful ways for you to know the truth about situations and people in your life, and to unlock the magical abilities within you to use your heart and your intuition to lead you in the right direction.

There's Value
in Every
Experience

Have you ever wanted to kill someone? Have you ever had that thought, even for just one second? As deeply painful as this is to admit, I did want to kill someone once—and I almost went through with it. If it had been as easy as pushing a "death button" and never being discovered or punished, I'm pretty sure I would have done it.

The person I almost killed was my mother. And although it's very difficult to think about it now—and even harder to share this story with you—in retrospect, I think that the experience taught me an immensely valuable lesson worth sharing.

It began one day in my late teens when I was suffering from very severe stomach cramps. I was curled up in a ball, lying in bed with my arms wrapped around my abdomen and trying to will away the pain. At times the cramps were so acute that it was hard for me to breathe. It felt as if every breath I took brought a more intense wave of pain, like a knife was being jammed into my gut.

I was in my freshman year at college and visiting my mother for a long weekend. She was often unstable and had been in and out of hospitals for paranoia and schizophrenia. When I arrived, she was in a good mood, and I was relieved. She was often very violent—once she was even placed in a state mental ward because doctors were worried that she might be capable of severely injuring or killing me.

Growing up, there were four of us (my sister, my two brothers, and me), but perhaps because I was the oldest, my mother seemed to especially take her rage out on me. When I was a child, it wasn't uncommon for her to lash out unexpectedly—for example, late at night, she'd become angry about some infraction she'd imagined that I'd committed. While I was sleeping, she'd storm into my bedroom, flip on the light, and yank off my covers. Then she'd wail and scream in an animal-like voice, as she flung her tightly clenched fists at my body again and again, hitting me as hard as she could.

My usual defense was to protect my head by curling up in the fetal position and wait for her to wear herself out. I never fought back—I just tried to survive these occasional onslaughts. As a child, I put up with it, partly because she was my mother, partly because I knew she was mentally ill, and partly because I believed that I must have deserved it in some way.

Even though my mother was cheerful when I first arrived for this particular visit, her state rapidly deteriorated as soon as I got the stomach cramps. Being under the weather when I was growing up was always a challenge because sometimes my mother would be caring and bring me hot chocolate and Jell-O and stroke my head—but other times, she'd think that I was pretending to be sick in order to sabotage her in some way or to undermine her authority. When she felt that way, it wasn't unusual for her to become violent, even if I was very ill.

As I writhed in agony on the bed, I could tell what kind of mood she was in . . . and I was afraid. She was strong and quick, and my cramps were so severe that I didn't know if I could stand up, let alone outrun her if she began hitting me. When she approached and started making her howling noises, I wanted to flee but didn't seem to have the strength to run. Instead, I reverted to my childhood defense posture of curling up and grasping my head in my arms. As she slugged me over and over again, the pain from her blows *and* the cramps became as sharp as a bloodied spear thrust repeatedly into an enemy's gut . . . and something inside me snapped.

A rage exploded from inside me that seemed to boom through the ceiling and walls. Everything that I had endured living with her violence and insanity for so many years—and everything that I'd suppressed to maintain peace at all costs—erupted. I flew out of bed, grabbed my mother by her hair, and threw her down on the floor.

Straddling her body and holding her arms down with the weight of my legs, I pulled her hair as hard as I could with both hands. I yanked her head up and was about to smash it into the floor when in a flash of a second, an inner voice said, *If you slam her head on the floor, you might kill her. Are you ready for that?* My arms started to shake. *Yes! I want her dead! Yes! I want her to stop hitting me and yelling at me! I want to kill her!*

Are you sure you want to kill her? Are you willing to live with the consequences?

Consequences? Suddenly, a window opened to the future: I saw my life, as it would unfold from that moment forward, if I killed my mother. In my vision I was a grown woman, but in everyone else's eyes, I was known as the girl who had killed her mother. It would be with me always. Was it worth the consequences? I wasn't sure. I didn't want to let go of her hair—I wanted to yell, "I don't care!" and smash her head down again and again until she stopped breathing.

But the reality was, I *did* care.

I held her down, with my face was a few inches from hers and my trembling fingers clutching her long hair, and she smiled at me. It wasn't a kind, forgiving smile, as if she understood my pain. It was a sly, almost devious, smile as if she somehow had me exactly where she wanted me.

For a moment I was disoriented. And then I realized, *Oh my God! She wants me to hurt her!* I instantly let go of her, ran outside, and flung myself down under a tree. I was in shock—I couldn't understand why she'd want me to do something so horrible. Was it to end the pain she felt from being mentally ill? Was she trying to manipulate me to do it for her because she couldn't do it to herself? I didn't know. My mother had nearly taken her own life a number of times, but she'd never gone through with it. Even when she slit her wrist, she did it when we were all home and just ended up in a hospital for a few days.

I sat there under the tree, as haunting words echoed over and over again in my head: *I almost killed my mother! I almost killed my mother! I almost killed my mother!* I was numb for hours and could barely talk or think straight. So often I'd imagined how much better my life would be without her, and I'd come so close . . . too close . . . but now I wasn't sure that was what I really wanted.

I didn't tell anyone about this event—not even my own siblings—for more than 30 years. I carried around the guilt I felt about it through my entire life, too ashamed to admit to others that I'd been potentially capable of such an act. Then slowly, over time, I realized that I needed to forgive myself. I went back in my memory to visit myself as a young girl who'd gone through such emotional and physical pain, and who'd borne it so stoically. I imagined telling her that what had happened was understandable, considering what she'd had to endure. I told her that she was a good person who had nothing to be ashamed for, and then I took her in my arms and let her know that everything was all right. I told her that all was forgiven. And at that moment, a feeling of forgiveness flooded through me.

A few years after that, I discovered a positive and unexpected aspect of this difficult event in my life. I was teaching a weekend workshop in Helsinki, Finland, to a packed audience of more than 500, most of whom didn't speak English. With the assistance of a translator, I was just about to begin to address the crowd when I became aware of a man shuffling into the room. He was a big, bulky guy with the physique of a dockworker. His head drooped forward, and his thickset hands hung limply at his sides as he walked. His shoulders sagged and his entire body faltered forward with every step, as if he were carrying an unstable boulder on his back. I watched him laboriously drag himself across the room until he found a seat in the last row in the back.

At the end of the day, there was a long line of people waiting to ask me questions. I noticed that the man who'd come in late was reluctantly hanging back at the end of the line. After everyone had left, the two of us were alone in the room with the translator. He finally approached me and started to sob. I stood next to him quietly until he stopped. Then, through my translator, he told me that he'd gone to prison for many years . . . *for murdering his mother.*

The man told me that although he'd served his time and was now forgiven by society, there was not a minute in which he was able to forgive himself. For decades his shame and guilt had tortured him every moment of his life. He explained that during the guided meditation I'd led that day, his mother had spontaneously appeared before him, bathed in radiant, glowing light. She held her hand out to him and said, "Son, all is forgiven. I love you . . . always and forever." He explained to me that in that instant, the heaviness inside of him had vanished.

His eyes sparkled as he told me about this, and he said, "I know that I'm truly forgiven. I know that my mother loves me. Thank you so much." As he turned and walked out of the room, I watched him move with a certainty and a strength that he hadn't possessed when he entered the room. He held his head high and carried himself with grace. Tears streamed down my cheeks, and I glanced at the translator, who was also crying. Watching this man leave, I was grateful for the miracle I'd witnessed.

I also felt that I understood him in a very personal way. Due to my past experience with my own mother, I wasn't appalled by what this man had done because I'd been in his shoes. I felt nothing but immense compassion and acceptance for him. I didn't know his particular circumstances, yet I was so grateful that I could be supportive of him in his journey to wholeness. I even wondered if perhaps, in a strange way, it was *because* of my acceptance of myself for almost causing *my* mother's demise that the Divine act of forgiveness could occur for this man. Perhaps my own self-acceptance had created an accepting atmosphere during the meditation in which he could forgive himself.

EVERY EXPERIENCE ALLOWS YOU TO GROW

Self-forgiveness starts by understanding that you're on the planet to grow spiritually. Spirit doesn't care how comfortable or happy you are, just as long as you grow, until eventually you learn that you don't need to suffer to grow. Every single experience that you've had—even the ones that you judge as "bad" or "shameful"—are a part of your journey to wholeness, joy, and to the unconditional acceptance of self. When you understand this, you can begin to accept and forgive yourself and others for the difficult events of the past. As horrifying as the experience of almost killing my mother was for me, it gave me compassion for other people who might be dealing with guilt of any kind . . . even the shame of killing someone else. I could have been in the same circumstance had I not run out of the house, something for which I'm eternally grateful.

Over the years I've learned the value of forgiving ourselves for *any* incident that we feel guilty about—not just the seemingly huge ones. Anything that negatively affects the way we feel about ourselves diminishes our being. For instance, if you forgot to pick up your kids from school one day (as I've done), or if you missed an important appointment because you were doing something you shouldn't have, it's time to forgive yourself. If there are other incidents that are causing you to still blame yourself, no matter how small, it's time to let them go.

Of course, this doesn't mean that you shouldn't take responsibility for your actions—you should. (Taking responsibility is an act of power and is different from continuing to blame yourself or feeling ashamed.) You should make amends for any misdeeds and do whatever you can to make it right. Feeling guilty doesn't fix anything, but taking action in the right direction can help. Also, by taking responsibility and accepting and loving yourself more deeply, you'll be able to accept and love others more deeply. It's impossible to truly love and accept something in another person that you can't love and accept within yourself.

STEPS TO EMPOWERMENT

What have you done in your life that makes you feel ashamed? List it all—write down absolutely everything, no matter how insignificant you judge it, or how totally embarrassed and guilty it makes you feel. After you've made your list, take time with each experience. You may want to go back in time in your mind and imagine yourself standing next to this younger version of yourself (even if the experience on your list happened only yesterday, you were less wise then). Spend time with this person, explaining that you feel infinite compassion for him or her, and let this younger you know that he or she is completely forgiven.

Additionally, look for ways that these experiences have allowed you to become more compassionate. Next to your list of shameful events from your past, write down what you learned or how you grew from them. This exercise can help replace your feelings of guilt with ones of gratitude for the older, stronger, wiser, more compassionate person you are today.

Appreciate It All

I opened the door and rushed inside the crowded bookstore. Finally, I was able to unbutton my coat. It had been tightly wrapped around my shoulders to ward off the damp chill outside that was growing colder with the setting of the sun.

As part of a lengthy book tour, I'd been scheduled to speak at a Barnes & Noble. Making my way past numerous rows of magazines and scattered tables with signs that read GREAT GIFT IDEAS and NEW RELEASES, I arrived in the middle of the store, where 40 chairs had been neatly set out for my talk. At the front, there was a table with a pitcher of water and a small drinking glass, along with a huge stack of my books that were all ready for me to autograph for the attendees. I set my belongings down at the table, next to an enlarged photograph of my smiling face that had been placed on an easel. The handwritten sign tacked to the poster read: DENISE LINN, 7 P.M.

I glanced at my watch. It was nearly time for the talk to begin, but no one else had arrived yet. I fiddled with my notes and tried to look interested in a book on the lighthouses of North America that I'd grabbed from a nearby shelf. I'd been admiring a photo of the one in Cape Elizabeth, Maine, when I looked up and noticed two women sitting in the last row of chairs. Realizing that it was already after 7:00, I put down the book, took a sip of water, and prepared to give my presentation.

This is certainly not as many people as I would have imagined, but these two women went out of their way to be here, I thought gallantly. *I really want to honor their effort, so I'm going to give my talk as if it were a packed house.*

I started by explaining the value of feng shui, the central topic of my new book, and how it could be applied to any home. I gave real-life examples of how the practice had affected people in positive and lasting ways, and I even showed charts and drawings to illustrate the ideas I was presenting. With an upbeat tone of voice, I tried to be as enthusiastic as I would have been had there been hundreds of people assembled instead of just two.

After finishing my lecture and feeling quite satisfied that I'd achieved my goal, I walked toward the two women to greet them and answer any questions they may have had about the book or my comments. As I reached them, however, they gave each other a sidelong glance and then looked down at the floor, as if to avoid making eye contact with me.

"Thanks for coming, ladies. Is there anything I can elaborate on for you?" I asked with a touch of reserve, wondering if I'd overpowered them during my talk with my enthusiasm.

After clearing her throat, the less demure of the two looked up hesitantly and said, "Um, well, actually we didn't come here for your talk. We've been in here shopping for a while, and we'd just sat down for a moment's rest when you started your talk. I'm afraid that we were a bit too embarrassed to leave."

My heart sank to the floor. I was mortified, but I thanked them for their candor as they gathered their things to leave.

I wish I could say that this was the only time in my life that I felt that kind of embarrassment, but unfortunately, it wasn't . . . in fact, it's happened lots of times. There was the time when I was in my early 20s and living in Hawaii, for instance, and some friends invited me to a gathering at their home on April 16th in honor of some obscure holiday.

Since April 16th is my birthday and all my pals were going to be there, I was sure that the real purpose of the gathering was a surprise party for me. My sister had planned to take me out that evening, but I told her that my friends were planning a party for me. Unfortunately, I couldn't invite her because I had to pretend that I didn't know what they were up to.

That afternoon I took the bus into Honolulu and bought a new outfit for my "party." I treated myself to a beautiful silk top in petal pink—just the right thing for such a festive occasion. Intrigued by the window display in a local salon, I decided to splurge and have my hair cut. It had been a while, and what could be a better excuse for a trim than a party where I was to be the guest of honor? And back at my house, I was almost finished getting ready when I decided to manicure my fingernails with P. Shine, a fancy Japanese product that I'd bought a few months earlier but had been saving for a special event.

I'd never had a surprise party before; I was so excited that I could hardly wait for the moment to come. All day I kept imagining how I was going to feign shock when everyone shouted, "Surprise!" I even practiced a few times in front of the mirror to make sure that I was believable.

When I arrived at the party and realized that my entrance hadn't resulted in shouts of surprise, I figured that the guests must have come up with a more original idea. I kept waiting for an announcement or the moment when everyone would bring out the presents. But then 8 P.M. rolled by . . . and then 9 P.M. . . . and then people started leaving! They were going before the birthday cake came and before I opened their presents!

Then it hit me. This *wasn't* a party for me—it was, in fact, just a gathering. The entire time I was thinking that people were pretending to forget my birthday, when, as it turned out, they actually *had* forgotten. I immediately slipped on my coat and crept out without even saying good-bye. The worst part was the shame I felt at declining my sister's invitation to celebrate my birthday so that I could go to what I considered a better option . . . my big surprise "party."

Another more recent example of humiliation came during a family vacation to Cabo San Lucas, Mexico, over the Christmas holidays. In an attempt to be thrifty, I'd decided to look online for an inexpensive hotel. During my search I'd come across a motel nestled in the heart of the city instead of near the ocean. I was a bit concerned because it wasn't by the sea and didn't have a swimming pool, but the price was right. And when I called the motel's manager to inquire about his establishment, he assured me that I could have the best of both worlds if I stayed there. He said that all of the beach resorts invited guests from outside hotels to use their pools and their beach access because they made money on drinks. It sounded reasonable, so I prepaid for the bargain room and congratulated myself on a job well done.

When my husband, David; daughter, Meadow; and I arrived in Cabo San Lucas on Christmas Eve, the situation looked grim, for this wasn't the tropical paradise I'd imagined. We quickly realized that our motel was inexpensive not only because it didn't have a pool and was miles from the teal blue water, but because it was located next to several factories, too. Perhaps if we'd been lucky enough to have a room facing the inner courtyard, it wouldn't have been so bad—instead, our stuffy, fluorescent-lit room looked out at a noisy, unpaved city street.

As we unsuccessfully tried to sleep that first night, large diesel trucks idled noisily a few feet outside our room, and to make matters worse, the air-conditioning unit in our room was broken, and an off-balance, overhead fan squeaked relentlessly. Across the road was a tortilla factory that operated throughout the night—it also had several big dogs tied up in front that barked incessantly into the early hours of the morning. When we opened the window to get air, the jarring sound of the barking dogs and the overpowering fumes of diesel oil combined with whiffs of garbage filled the room. When we closed the window, the room became too hot to bear.

Unable to sleep, David and Meadow started voicing their disappointment with the accommodations I'd chosen. Even though it felt like the night that would never end, I tried to reassure my family by reminding them about the oceanfront-hotel policy that allowed other vacationers to use their pools and beaches.

"Don't worry," I said. "Tomorrow's going to be great. And all we have to do is sleep here—we'll be so tired from spending our days at the beach hotels that we'll just collapse in bed despite the noise."

The next day was Christmas. David decided to stay in bed since he hadn't gotten much rest during the night, while Meadow and I planned a morning trek to one of the massive hotels overlooking the sea. We walked to the beach and found a nice hotel, where we dropped our bags and settled in by the pool.

At last we were on vacation! I was finally relaxing, taking in the astonishing view of the ocean, when a hotel employee approached my daughter and me and asked to have a word. He pulled us aside, explaining that he was the assistant manager and if we weren't guests of the hotel, we had no business being on the property, so we'd have to leave immediately. He waited while we awkwardly gathered all of our things and more or less unceremoniously escorted us off the premises. We were treated like criminals trying to get away with something—like shoplifters caught on tape.

This scenario replayed itself at several other beach hotels before I realized that we'd been victims of a lie told by our motel's manager in order to get us to book accommodations at his establishment. (I wished that I'd listened with my heart instead of hearing what I *wanted* to hear.) We learned the hard way that oceanfront hotels were *not* delighted to have people who weren't guests sit by their pools or frequent their beaches.

The worst part of the humiliation was seeing Meadow's fallen face when we were "found out." Her embarrassment struck me right in the stomach, leaving me with a heavy, sick feeling. It was hard to be disgraced like that in front of my daughter . . . especially on Christmas. It was even worse to see her humiliated as a result of my actions. She did manage to give me a half smile, as she quietly uttered, "No room at the inn," reassuring me that she was okay.

As we walked back to our tortilla-factory motel, I talked to Meadow about what had happened. I told her to always remember how it felt to be humiliated because it could help her empathize with the plight of others, especially those who had to deal with degradation as a part of everyday life. We admitted how fortunate we both were because mortification was an unusual occurrence for us, and we pledged to remember those feelings and to cherish the wisdom that came from what we'd gone through.

CHERISH *EVERY* EXPERIENCE

As challenging as the humiliating situations I've shared with you in this chapter were at the time, I'm very grateful to have had them throughout my life. I have a strengthened sense of self and a deeper compassion for the plight of others because of events such as speaking passionately to two uninterested bookstore shoppers, anticipating the surprise party that never happened, and getting kicked off the beach in Mexico. I may have been humiliated, embarrassed, or degraded in my life, but each time I've learned so much, and for this I am grateful.

In life, there are times when we'll be treated poorly or unfairly or will be humiliated publicly—it's the nature of being alive. You can choose to shove these experiences under a rock and try to forget them, or you can embrace them and let them shape your evolution. I'm not one to vote for suffering as a way to build character, but if you've ever endured a situation similar to the ones I've mentioned here, then know that it can deepen your compassion for others and make you a kinder human being.

It can be very difficult to connect with someone else's heart if you haven't connected to your own, and it's nearly impossible to have compassion for the pain of others if you haven't embraced it within yourself first. So rather than resenting a difficult situation for making you feel hurt or belittled, cherish it, and take it upon yourself to turn the humiliating experience into an event that can hold power and meaning for you in the journey ahead.

STEPS TO EMPOWERMENT

What have been some of *your* most humiliating moments? On a sheet of paper, list as many as you can. Spend time thinking about each event: Were you indoors or out? What was the scenery like? Were you warm or were you cold? Who was with you? What scents were in the air? What were you wearing? Take the time to fully re-create the scene in your mind. Really feel the shame/humiliation/degradation/embarrassment that you felt at the time.

As you go back and relive these difficult experiences, think about what you learned and in what ways these events can help you become more compassionate and understanding, and write it down on your piece of paper. If you don't think that these experiences have any value in your life, make another list and write all the ways that these events could *potentially* help you in the future. Once you've done so, be willing to cherish your experiences—because not only have they helped you become who you are today, they can also help mold who you'll become in the future.

The Power of Knowing Your Ultimate Goal

It was almost summer vacation and my daughter, Meadow, who was in the fourth grade, was already worried about starting fifth grade that coming September. "Mom, I'm really afraid to start school next year," she said, tears welling up in her eyes.

"What makes you say that, honey?" I asked, feeling a bit alarmed.

"Mr. Bates makes his fifth graders do push-ups when they're bad, and I can't even do one," she whispered in a trembling voice.

"You're a good student, Meadow. This won't be a problem for you," I assured her.

She still looked very concerned. For the next few days her eyebrows were furrowed into two deep lines, and she looked like she was carrying a bundle of rocks on her skinny little shoulders. I could tell that she was really scared of this Mr. Bates, and I didn't want her fear to escalate over the summer, so I decided to arrange an informal get-together with the two of them. I didn't mention Meadow's worries to him—I just said that I wanted to get to know him before she started his class in the fall.

As we sat in her soon-to-be teacher's classroom and chatted amicably with him, my daughter looked down at the floor and barely contributed to the conversation. But when we walked through the playground toward the car, Meadow admitted that even though she was still a little afraid of him, she did feel better about having him for her teacher.

I was still really concerned about her fear, so I said, "You will not be punished in Mr. Bates's class. I absolutely promise that this will never happen to you." As soon those words left my lips, her shoulders relaxed and she smiled, because she knew that I would never lie to her. I felt confident telling her this because she was a good student, and her teachers always said that she was well mannered in class. Mr. Bates's name didn't come up again for the rest of the summer, but I did see her occasionally practicing push-ups in the hallway.

On one of the first days of fifth grade, I noticed that as Meadow came up from the bus stop, her face was pale and drawn and her eyes were red. As soon as she saw me, she burst into tears.

"What happened?" I pleaded.

Sobbing, she divulged, "I got in trouble, and Mr. Bates made me do push-ups on the floor during class."

"Why did he do this?" I demanded, trying to sound calm.

She explained that he'd given two orders in quick succession. The first command for the class was to turn to page 54 in their book, and the second instruction was to look up at him. Meadow didn't realize that he actually wanted them to look up at him immediately, so she was still trying to find page 54 when Mr. Bates bellowed at her, "Meadow Linn! You didn't look up at me when I told you to! Get down on the floor and do three push-ups!"

She said that she'd felt so ashamed as she got up from her desk and began doing the push-ups. She really struggled because she wasn't strong enough to actually do them.

I remembered my words to her that previous summer—I'd assured her that she'd *never* be punished in that class. I'd promised! And now she'd received a punishment and been humiliated in front of her classmates. I knew that I probably shouldn't have given her my word, since whatever was to happen in the classroom was out of my control, but I was just so confident that something like this would never happen to her.

How could a teacher be so cruel? I wondered. The more I thought about it, the more a rage began to build inside of me, until it ignited like wildfire and roared through my entire body. I left Meadow with a friend who was staying with us, sprinted to my car, turned the key, and floored it out of the driveway. It was all I could do to keep the vehicle under control as I raced toward the school.

I skidded to a halt in the parking lot and charged up the front steps, screaming, "Where is Mr. Bates?! *Where is he?!* I'm going to get him!" I ran from one empty room to another, hollering at the top of my lungs. The janitor looked shocked, and a few people peered out of their offices. I had my fist clenched in preparation. *I promised Meadow that this would never happen! How could a teacher be so unfair?*

I searched every classroom until I came to the conclusion that he wasn't in the main building, so I headed toward some of the other school buildings, yelling, "Where's Robert Bates?!"

Another teacher stepped out of an empty classroom, looked at me, and calmly stated, "I believe he's gone home for the day."

"Where does he live?!" I demanded.

She was an older teacher, probably in her early 60s, with gray hair and a warm face full of wrinkles and smile lines. She'd probably been teaching for more than 30 years and was adept at dealing with irate parents, so she smiled serenely and said, "I can tell you where he lives, but please come into my classroom for a moment first and let me know what happened. Maybe I can help." She put her hand on my back and ushered me into her room.

The woman listened openly and kindly, even agreeing that the way Mr. Bates went about disciplining the children was questionable and had raised some concerns in the past. She assured me that she'd bring the situation up with school authorities at the next meeting. Then she lowered her voice and narrowed her eyes.

"Mrs. Linn, I know that you're upset, and rightfully so, but if you attack Mr. Bates, you'll probably be charged with assault," she said seriously, yet gently. "Meadow may even have to withdraw from this school. What you'd like to do might be momentarily satisfying, but in the long run, I think you might regret it. Sometimes the pen is mightier than the sword—why don't you write to him and express your concerns?" As she spoke, I could tell that her consideration for both my daughter and me was genuine.

Once she calmed me down, I realized how fortunate I was that Mr. Bates hadn't been at the school that afternoon. I would have been deeply remorseful had I lashed out at him, no matter how mad I might have been. I was also ashamed that I'd lost control.

What kind of example am I for Meadow? I thought with a pang of guilt.

When I got home, I took some time to talk to Meadow, who was having tea with my friend. I apologized for racing out of the house so quickly, and I stressed that violence is never the way to solve disagreements. I promised my daughter that I'd be a better example for her and that I'd *talk* about the problems I faced, rather than yelling about them.

We also spoke about the possibility that sometimes the things we most fear are the very things we attract. Although I emphasized that Meadow absolutely didn't deserve what happened to her, I suggested that perhaps her worrying about Mr. Bates had helped create the situation. I used the example of someone carrying a very full glass of water—a person who's overly preoccupied that he might spill it is much more likely to have the water slosh out of the glass than someone who visualizes every drop staying in the glass. I told her to focus on her ultimate positive outcome rather than putting her attention on what she was afraid of.

I then explained that we have the power to attract what we focus on, so we have to be careful that the things that command our attention aren't negative or what we fear. My daughter confessed that she'd been so afraid that Mr. Bates would punish her that she'd practiced doing push-ups over the summer because she knew that this was one of his favorite punishments. Unfortunately, she hadn't been too successful in mastering the exercise due to her slight build. She admitted the possibility that her fear *had* contributed to what happened, because it had certainly been on her mind a lot. We then talked about focusing on something positive: We visualized her having fun in class and coming home from school the next day feeling wonderful.

After Meadow went to bed, I sat down to write a letter to Mr. Bates. Before I started, I took the advice I'd given Meadow. (I believe that the advice that we give others is often what we need ourselves. Many times I find myself teaching others what I need to learn myself.) I focused on the outcome that I hoped to achieve by writing the letter. Although it might have been momentarily gratifying to blast him for being so callous, I knew that my satisfaction would be short-lived. It would be more satisfying if my letter actually made an impact on Mr. Bates—I hoped that my words might prevent Meadow, or any other child for that matter, from having to endure such a humiliating experience ever again.

With that intention in mind, I wrote the best letter I'd ever written. It was a thoughtful, well-considered missive in which I detailed my respect for educators, giving examples of how important my elementary school teachers had been in my childhood and how I still carried their wisdom with me in everyday life. I said that in our busy world, a child often spends more hours with her teachers than with her parents. I recognized the awesome responsibility that a teacher has in shaping a child's self-esteem, and I reaffirmed how the effect of a good teacher dramatically influences how a young person perceives herself through adulthood.

I went on to recognize the importance of using discipline in the classroom, acknowledging how difficult it must be at times to keep order among unruly kids. But then I talked about how humiliation is used in the military to tear down the individuality of a person in order to subjugate his will to his commanders. Although this strategy is necessary for a disciplined fighting force, I explained that children, unlike grown men and women, could suffer serious damage to their confidence when forced to endure demeaning punishments.

I didn't make any demands or ask Mr. Bates to change what he was doing—I just wrote a well-crafted, logical letter. I attempted to look at the world through his eyes, while sharing my perception at the same time. With every word I wrote, I kept a vision in my mind of my ultimate goal. I sent my letter, and a week later I received a brief, cursory note that thanked me for writing. I wasn't sure if I'd gotten through to him or not.

As several teachers would later reveal to me, a miracle happened. In spite of 15 years of using the same disciplinary methods, Mr. Bates never again used push-ups to punish a child. And Meadow had one of the best years at elementary school and talks about Mr. Bates with fondness to this day. Years later, I was told that he still managed to maintain order in his classroom without reverting to his old humiliating tactics—and I believe that he changed because of the letter I wrote. I was proud of myself for my willingness to let go of my anger and my temptation to prove I was right, and to write a thought-provoking letter instead of a self-righteous one. I also felt good for keeping the focus on creating a better classroom environment not only for my daughter, but for *all* the kids who'd sit in his classroom over the years.

WHAT'S YOUR ULTIMATE GOAL?

When you get into an argument or a disagreement with others, ask yourself if your ultimate goal is to be right . . . or to get results. Instead of trying to convince someone else that you're right and they're wrong—which almost never works anyway—a better strategy is to concentrate on your goal. Ask yourself, *Is my focus on being right or on getting results? What's my ultimate goal here, and what do I need to do or say to achieve it? What can I do to bring this to a positive resolution?* These types of questions will propel you away from the need to be judgmental and indignant, and toward the results you desire.

A few days ago, I witnessed an example of what can happen when you keep your attention on being right rather than on your ultimate goal. I was shopping at a small grocery store and overheard a woman whining to the manager of the meat department about some fish that she'd purchased there. She complained in a high-pitched voice about how it "smelled up" her kitchen. The manager got defensive, and the discussion escalated into an argument until the woman finally stormed off. She was still fuming as she stood behind me in line to pay for her other groceries. We started talking, and in the course of the conversation I asked what would have made her happy regarding the situation. She answered, "I wanted to get my money back or have them give me fresher fish free of charge, of course." I was amazed at how little of what she'd yelled at the manager actually related to getting her goal. It was more about proving that she'd been wronged.

Remarkably, this woman's comments reminded me of another time I'd been at that same store. Standing in line to get some fish myself, I'd overheard a woman at the counter mention to the meat manager how much she enjoyed shopping at that store, and how much she appreciated the good quality and value she found there. She mentioned that she'd gotten some meat that was just a little off, however, and she wondered if she could get a replacement or a refund. The manager grinned from ear to ear and answered, "I'm so sorry to hear that. Unfortunately, it happens sometimes, but we're always happy to accommodate our customers." I watched as he wrapped up several big steaks, much more than she'd originally purchased, and wrote No Charge on the outside of the package.

Interestingly, both women had the same goal. However, the first woman wasted time trying to be right and didn't focus on her desired outcome. The second woman, on the other hand, was very clear on her desired outcome and went home with a package of fresh steaks. If I'd written a letter to Mr. Bates ranting about how outraged *I* was and how wrong *he* was, I doubt that the situation would have ever changed. Writing to him as I did, with a clear idea of my desired outcome and without blame or shame, I was able to get my point across. And it was probably much easier for him to accept what I had to say and to think about changing the way he treated his students.

The lesson I learned from these instances is that by focusing on your desired result, rather than on venting your anger or trying to prove that you're right, the more likely it is that you'll achieve your goal.

Steps to Empowerment

Take a look at the events that are part of your upcoming day and ask yourself, *What's my desired outcome?* For example, if you plan on having a conversation with a friend over coffee, maybe your ultimate goal is to feel joy. If you're driving to work, your outcome might be to get to your job, but it also might be to have an enjoyable drive or to learn something by listening to the radio. At the beginning of each day, consider writing down a list of your activities, along with what your desired outcome is for each event.

Then take the time to imagine what you'll need to create to obtain this outcome. Where your intention goes, your energy flows, and doing this exercise will help you reach your goals.

Another exercise is one that you can do at the beginning of each day. Simply ask yourself, *What's my ultimate goal or desired outcome for the overall events of this day?* Then ask yourself a second question: *Is this really what I want?*

The second question is important because sometimes we answer the first question with our mind, but the second question is often answered with our heart. This morning, for instance, when I asked myself what outcome I desired for the day, my first answer was to be productive and accomplish a substantial amount of writing. But when I asked myself, *Is this really what I want?* I took time to be still and listen to my soul. I realized that my ultimate outcome was to feel relaxed and spend time in the garden with my chickens, as well as be productive with my writing. Since I made sure that both of these things were a part of my day, I felt very satisfied and successful.

The more you keep focused on your ultimate outcome for any given day, and then design your life toward that goal, the more likely you are to feel deep satisfaction at the day's conclusion.

⁓

Indulge Yourself
with Joy
Instead of Guilt

All I could think about was that basement. For some reason, we kids were forbidden from going into it—nevertheless, all I could think about was how deliciously cool and dark it was down there, especially since it was such a hot summer afternoon. I was five years old; my sister, Heather, was three; and we were sitting on the front steps of our house, sweltering in the central California sun. It was the kind of heat that pervades every part of your being and makes even doing nothing seem like too much effort. But I just kept thinking about the basement.

Even though we weren't allowed to go there, I convinced Heather that we could sneak in, cool off, and be back outdoors before anyone found out. This could especially work if we used the outside door that led to the basement. Heather was unsure, but as only big sisters can do, I convinced her that it would be fine and tugged her along. When we got to the door, I took a quick look in both directions to make sure that no one saw us go in, and then we slipped inside.

There was a small room at the far end of the basement that had a freezer in it. With my sister close behind, I walked purposefully into that back room, swung open the freezer door, and let the icy air billow out and chill my face. It felt good—no, it felt *great!*

"We're not supposed to open the door. It'll let all the cold out," said Heather, who was an obedient child and was always concerned about doing the right thing.

My only motivation, however, was the refreshing coolness of the freezer air and how exciting it was to be there. "Hey, it's okay.

We won't tell anyone. Besides, you're hot, aren't you? C'mere, I'll show you how to cool off—it's easy. You just put your tongue on the frost. Go ahead . . . try it."

"You do it first," Heather squeaked.

"Okay, I will." And I stuck my tongue out and pushed it up against the large layer of frost that lined the freezer shelf. At first it felt delightful, just a little colder than I had anticipated. Then I tried to pull away, but found that I couldn't. My tongue was stuck to the frosty ice.

"'elp! 'elp!" I cried, "I 'an't 'et my 'ongue off. Go get 'elp, 'eather!"

"No!" she was adamant.

"Go get 'elp," I tried to say, my words becoming muffled as my tongue became more and more frozen to the shelf. I was starting to panic, and it was hard to swallow with my tongue hanging out.

"No! I'm not going to. We're not supposed to be in here. We'll get in trouble!" Heather whined, sporting the determined look that told me she wasn't going to budge.

Realizing that my sister wasn't going to go get help, I put both hands on the door and yanked my head back with all the strength my desperation could produce. "Ow!" I cried. I could taste the blood beading up on my tongue.

My gigantic yelp scared Heather so much that she started screaming, too. Suddenly she became quiet as her eyes caught sight of the freezer shelf. I turned to see what she was looking at and spied an almost perfect circle of bloody skin still stuck to the ice. The shock of seeing this was so surprising that I ceased to notice the pain in my tongue. As we slowly edged closer to examine it, I tentatively reached out and touched it. It felt cold and slimy.

We were filled with both fascination and horror. That little patch of skin was an awesome sight! The next day, we even snuck a couple of neighborhood kids down to see it.

I'd like to say that I never touched my tongue to the frost again, but the allure of the coolness of the freezer on hot days was too enticing. Eventually there was a small row of meaty red circles on the freezer shelf. Somehow the pain of losing a bit of skin was worth the forbidden pleasure of the coolness of the ice on my tongue.

Later that summer, when my mother was entertaining some friends at the house, I overheard her remark, "It's really curious—there are strange-looking red circles on the freezer shelf downstairs. I can't imagine what they are or how they got there."

THE ALLURE OF FORBIDDEN PLACES AND GUILTY PLEASURES

Even as a child, I wanted to explore forbidden places, even if it wasn't always to my advantage. As an adult, I've come to accept that there are still things that I do that aren't good for my body or my soul, yet I continue to do them because they bring me such undeniable (if temporary) pleasure.

For example, my body feels much better when I don't drink alcohol—however, the sensation of a cold beer sliding down the back of my throat on a hot day feels like gliding on ice. The following morning, when I'm a little groggy, I usually berate myself and swear I'll never drink again. Yet when the next hot day rolls around, I inevitably grab a frosty brew again.

Movies are another area where this occurs for me. I always feel so much better when I watch a family film or a romantic comedy with a happy ending—bur there are times when I'm standing at the DVD-rental store and can't help but reach for a dark, violent, sexual thriller. I know that I'll probably have nightmares resulting from the content, but the allure is too great. Each time I promise myself that I'll never rent another disturbing movie again . . . ever! Nevertheless, when I'm saturated with feel-good flicks, I crave another blockbuster thriller.

Chocolate is another forbidden pleasure for me. I know that research has shown that a little bit of dark chocolate can be good for you—but no one said that you should eat the whole box! I once bought my daughter, Meadow, a pound of chocolates for Christmas. I wrapped it beautifully and put it away on a high shelf until Christmas. One night, in a moment of weakness, I got it down, tore it open, and ate the whole box. The next day I drove to the candy store to replace it. I wrapped up the new box and swore to myself that I'd never do something so stupid again. That promise lasted until I ripped *that* box open and gobbled down every piece. I did that three times altogether! I no longer buy chocolates for Meadow for Christmas.

My sexual fantasies are another taboo. I believe that a wholesome fantasy life is a sign of an active and healthy imagination—yet my favorite sexual fantasies don't tend to be romantic or spiritual . . . not even close. They're gutsy, earthy, and sometimes even lascivious. When I have one of these fantasies, I feel so guilty that I try to momentarily convince myself that I'm the only one who knows about them. I pretend that God, angels, or guides aren't really watching over me in that moment. But then later, I say, "Okay, just kidding. I know that you're there." On top of feeling guilty about my thoughts and fantasies, I also end up feeling guilty about denying my beliefs!

The question is: What is it about the forbidden that's so appealing? And why would I continue to do something that obviously isn't good for my mind, body, or spirit? I honestly don't know the full answer to that. I *do* know that, in spite of how hard I may try to resist, I still indulge in a number of guilty pleasures.

Given that I haven't been successful in curbing these yearnings, I've begun to wonder whether resisting them is even a good idea. I've come to the conclusion that enjoying these parts of my life without shame or judgment is really the healthier approach. Giving in a little bit here and there may actually be good for me—it's in going overboard with one of these indulgences where the danger might lie. So instead of the added shame of trying unsuccessfully to resist a forbidden pleasure, I occasionally indulge in it and try to enjoy it without guilt (or with as little guilt as possible). The strange thing about this philosophy is that the more I allow myself these pleasures without feeling bad or ashamed, the less I'm drawn to them. Their appeal seems to diminish once I've deemed them allowable.

This reminds me of one of my seminars, in which a woman lamented to me that for more than 35 years she'd tried absolutely everything to quit smoking, but nothing had worked. She asked what I suggested.

Thinking of my guilty-pleasure philosophy, I asked her if she liked to smoke. "No," she replied. "It's a nasty, dirty, horrible habit."

I responded, "I know that's what people tell you and that's what you're supposed to feel, but be honest with me. Do you enjoy smoking?"

Looking a bit abashed, she admitted, "I'm not sure . . . I feel so guilty every time I have a cigarette that all I'm aware of feeling is the guilt and shame."

"Then I have a suggestion for you. The next time you smoke, choose it. I mean really *choose it*. Decide that you're going to smoke, and enjoy your cigarette. Relish it."

"But I don't want to smoke anymore," she asserted.

"Well, if you've tried everything, as you said you have, and nothing's worked, then there might be a chance that you'll never stop smoking. Is that true?"

"But I want to quit."

"I know you want to—and you certainly might—but is it true that you may never quit?"

She looked at me for a long time and then quietly acknowledged, "Yes, it's true."

"So given that you may smoke for the rest of your life, don't you think that it would be better to enjoy smoking rather than rake yourself over the coals every time you light up?"

At first, she wasn't fully convinced that she could actually enjoy the dubious act of smoking, but finally she agreed to try to thoroughly relish every cigarette. A few months later, I received a letter from this woman saying that she'd taken my advice and had given herself permission to enjoy smoking. She said that an incredible thing had happened once she'd finally accepted herself as a smoker.

"I have much less need to do it," she wrote. "In fact, for the first time since I started smoking, I'm having only a couple cigarettes a day, as opposed to the *two packs* I was having before. To me, this is a miracle. You would have thought that as soon as I consciously chose to smoke I would have gone for it more, but the opposite has occurred. Amazingly, I'm losing my desire to smoke."

There's something to be learned here. First, let me be clear that I'm not advocating or encouraging any form of addiction. If you're doing something that's harming you and you can't stop, you should do everything you can to seek help overcoming it rather than indulging in it. This is another topic for discussion altogether, and I encourage you to keep trying to beat addiction. However, when you partake of your small guilty pleasures, let go of the shame and guilt as much as possible, and thoroughly enjoy these parts of your life. Consciously choose your life rather than be the victim of it.

STEPS TO EMPOWERMENT

What are *your* forbidden pleasures? Do you feel shame or guilt every time you indulge in them? Make a list of them and be willing to *consciously choose* to indulge in them rather than covertly beating yourself up and filling yourself with self-recrimination. And if you do find yourself feeling ashamed or guilty, then allow yourself to feel these emotions and even to cherish them rather than deny them. Perhaps your guilt is your forbidden pleasure!

If you can enjoy the choices you make in your life, even the ones you've considered shameful or have tried to suppress, you'll feel healthier about yourself and more in control of your own life.

VALUE YOUR "FAILURES"

I don't know how I got it into my head that I could do drama. In my typical manner of leap first, think later, when an opportunity came, I jumped first—and freaked out later.

While on a speaking tour that took me through the Netherlands, I met a Dutch director from Amsterdam. In the course of chatting with her, I mentioned that I'd done some acting (okay, so it had only been minor parts in the high school plays of my small farming town, but it was still acting . . . right?). When she offhandedly suggested that I do a one-woman show focusing on Native American stories, because of my Cherokee heritage I enthusiastically agreed. She said that she'd make the arrangements for it to coincide with my next trip to Holland. I was ecstatic. *How hard could it be? I'm always speaking in front of people on my seminar tours, so acting can't be that difficult,* I thought. *I can just show up and improvise something on the spur of the moment, the same way that I do my seminars, can't I?*

I had no idea how wrong I was.

Six months later, my husband, David, and I arrived back in Amsterdam, and the director met us at the airport. She said, "I'm delighted to tell you that we have a sold-out crowd for your play—it's standing room only." I nodded easily, since I was accustomed to speaking at sold-out seminars. Doing a play would surely be almost the same thing.

We drove directly to the theater to meet with the staff, and I was shocked to see a huge group waiting for me. Sound engineers, lighting technicians, a stage crew, a stage manager, a photographer, and video technicians had all turned up, waiting at attention like an army anticipating their battle plan. For the first time since I'd agreed to do the play, I started to feel the enormity of my undertaking. *Oh God—I'm not an actress!* I panicked. *I've never had any training. What was I thinking?*

The director got right to business and informed me, "The sound and lighting technicians and the stage manager need to know your cues. They're ready whenever you are."

My cues? I don't have any cues! I'd thought that the inspiration would occur onstage, in the moment. After all, in my lectures I never worked from a script. Yes, in a seminar it was sometimes unnerving to talk to an audience of hundreds of people without a plan, but the spontaneity and insight that occurred with this spur-of-the-moment technique had always worked for me. The end results seemed worth the uncertainty I often experienced before a lecture. But as I looked at the faces of the eager stage crew, I suddenly realized that a play was very different from a seminar. My high school experiences certainly hadn't prepared me for this kind of scenario.

I felt so stupid. I hadn't realized that I needed cues. Suddenly it hit me that I was in trouble. *Oh, no! I can't just show up and wing it. What in the world am I going to do?*

"Um, I'm a bit jet-lagged . . . could I possibly go out for a quick cup of tea and meet you back here in 30 minutes?" I inquired, trying to look calm, even as sweat trickled down the curve of my back. Everyone agreed, saying that they had other things they could do while they waited for me.

On the short walk to the café, I sobbed to David, "Damn! Damn! Damn! I'm so stupid. What was I thinking? How could I have been so dumb as to think that I could just show up and do a play with no script, no rehearsal, *and no plan?* I'm so scared." I berated myself all the way to the coffeehouse.

David just squeezed my hand and offered his pragmatic support, "Denise, just do the best you can. We have a few minutes right now to think of some cues. And then you have between now and tonight to come up with a script."

Together we came up with some great ideas, and I walked back to the theater feeling much more at ease. Even though it was a somewhat unconventional approach, everyone seemed satisfied as long as they had their cues. For example, I told the sound technicians that when they heard the words *go into the cave,* they should put reverb on my voice. I suggested to the lighting engineer that whenever I drummed, he could put a single spotlight on the drum and then fade it to my face. For my entrance, I even suggested blowing air across dry ice to simulate smoke flowing on to the stage. Although I tried to look as confident and rehearsed what I could, I felt like an imposter foolishly wasting the time and effort that went into putting together a play.

Later that night, I peeked out from the edge of the stage at the people filing into the theater. It was about 15 minutes before the performance, and my mouth was so dry that I couldn't swallow. *At least I have my frame drum and my Native American regalia,* I thought. *I can do some drumming—that will take up some time in my performance.* I picked up my drum and looked in horror as I saw the sagging skin in its center. The damp atmosphere of Amsterdam's below-sea-level location had caused the skin on the drumhead to loosen and droop. After much searching, I found two hair dryers and tried to manipulate the rawhide back into its taut position on the wooden frame. Unfortunately, it just continued to sag. I looked at it in dismay, wondering, *What am I going to do!* There were only four minutes until curtain time, so I was going to have to use it anyway.

I thought about bolting out of the theater and never coming back, but I knew I couldn't do that. The director would lose her reputation and a lot of money, and the audience might be angered. Once more I peered through the curtain at the crowd, and my heart beat as though it were going to thump right out of my chest. *God! Ancestors! Angels! Anyone up there! Help!* I prayed that someone—anyone—in the spirit world would listen to me and help.

When the curtain opened, I swallowed hard, took a deep breath, and slowly moved through the "fog" from the dry-ice machine toward the middle of the stage. It felt like a death walk. I clutched my drum so hard that the sinew actually started to cut into my hand. I then turned to look out into the audience, hoping to find a friendly face to connect with, as I'd usually done when giving seminar talks.

I can't see anyone! I thought in terror. The lights were so bright in my eyes that I was blinded! Even though the audience could see me, *I* couldn't see *them!* The image of an insect under a magnifying glass leapt into my mind. There was no friendly face or nodding head in the audience to which I could anchor myself—just a vast blackness before me. I was starkly alone on a stage . . . my arms couldn't move . . . my legs were frozen . . . and my throat felt like it had a lump of sawdust stuck in it.

Probably only a minute passed as I stood immobilized, but it felt like an hour. The ticking seconds seemed to loudly reverberate from one side of my brain to the other and back again. When I finally looked down, my arms appeared disconnected from my body. Somehow they slowly lifted my drum. During that period when time seemed to stand still, the drum skin had managed to tighten. I began to drum, slowly and intimately. As I heard the familiar sound, I relaxed a bit and began to sing my spirit songs—songs that had come to me during the long, lonely hours of my vision quests in nature. Everything and everyone was quiet as I sang. For a moment I wondered if anyone was really out there . . . but then I heard someone cough, and I was reminded that I wasn't alone.

Eventually I had the idea to have audience members come up and help me perform some of the Native American stories such as "Octopus Woman" and "How the Skunk Got Its Smell." For example, four members of the audience came onstage and stood behind one other in a line with their arms flailing around, pretending to be the Octopus Woman who uses flattery to entice unsuspecting passersby into the cold depths of the sea. (This is a traditional story from the Native Americans of the Northwest region of United States.) The audience seemed to enjoy participating in the show, and I found that I was less nervous if there were others up there with me.

Somehow I managed to survive the evening, even if at times I had the feeling that I was watching myself from a distance. Afterward, I plastered a smile on my face and thanked everyone—but when it was all over, I bolted out of the theater as fast as I could. I began to reflect on that evening's experience as I stumbled outside into the chilly night air.

Despite the applause that I'd received at the end of the show, I thought that everyone was just being polite. I was convinced they must have felt that this evening had been a waste of their time and money. Over and over again I kept saying to myself, *How could I have been so stupid? I should have had a script. I should have practiced.* I felt so miserable that I had trouble walking. I thought that I was going to pass out or throw up . . . or both. David held my arm as we walked so that I wouldn't trip on the cobbled streets.

When we got back to our hotel, I just lay on the bed unable to move. I'd managed to save myself and the director from humiliation, yet my performance felt like a failure. It had taken every ounce of energy I possessed in order to deal with a situation that I'd gotten myself into because I hadn't prepared for it. As I tried to recover in that hotel room, it seemed as if every breath took enormous effort. Although I'd gotten through the show, I felt that I'd let the director down. Even though she'd told me that my show was great, I was certain that I could read the disappointment in her eyes.

RETHINK THOSE SO-CALLED FAILURES

Failure isn't necessarily about what happens, it's how we *perceive* what happens. For example, on the evening of my one-woman show, I perceived that I'd failed—whether or not I'd actually done so by anyone else's standards was irrelevant. And while my sense of failure hadn't come from the audience responding in a negative way, *I* still felt deeply ashamed of my performance. I can't change what I felt at the time, but I *can* alter the way I view that experience as I look back on it now. For years my perception of failure was the only thing I'd remembered from the experience at the theater in Amsterdam; however, I've now come to realize that I also learned valuable life lessons that night.

I've learned that I'm strong enough to bounce back after what feels like failure. I also discovered that I have a great deal more courage than I thought I had, because I didn't run offstage in a panic (even though I wanted to). My theatrical debut also taught me the importance of preparation. If I'd planned ahead, I wouldn't have felt so hopeless and ashamed about my performance the night of the show. In addition, I've realized that if I'd let go of my attachment to my so-called failure, I would have recognized that I *did* get applause at the end of the night and that the compliments I received were undoubtedly sincere. (I was so attached to my negative viewpoint that I couldn't allow myself to experience the good things that happened that night.) So although my show seemed like a flop, I actually gained a lot that night.

I believe that you never truly know success until you've experienced failure, because with every downfall, you learn something. Thomas Edison tried thousands of different materials looking for a filament for the lightbulb. When he was asked if he was discouraged, he replied that he wasn't at all, because with each so-called failure, he discovered one more thing that wouldn't work. People who are successful do *not* have fewer failures than those who don't achieve success; in fact, sometimes they have more. It's not failure that separates successful individuals from those who aren't—it's the willingness to try new things, and to even fail at times, but to ultimately learn from each experience that helps define success.

Additionally, you can't really be a successful leader unless you know what it feels like to fail and you're not afraid of it. People who have to win at everything they attempt are often terrified of losing, and their fear diminishes their capacity to lead. If you're willing to fall on your face, you'll find that when you get back up and brush yourself off, you're stronger and wiser, and you've gained something of value. Every time you don't succeed, you also learn something—maybe what you learn is that you'll never to do it that way again, but perhaps you'll gain a new perspective that you can use in other areas of your life.

Steps to Empowerment

There is a simple exercise that you can do to help you turn your failures into successes. First, list five failures that you've experienced in your life. After each item, write what you learned from that experience. For example, I might list the Amsterdam play as one of my failures, and then underneath it I might list what I learned: (1) Preparation is important, (2) I have more courage than I give myself credit for, and (3) even if something is deeply embarrassing, I *can* live through it . . . and even laugh about it later.

If you're unable to do this exercise because you can't think of any failures, then it might be time to consider taking a few more risks. What's a risk that you could take today? Next week? Next month? Don't just think about it—schedule it! Write it into your calendar or day planner. Make an appointment with yourself, and challenge yourself to step out of your comfort zone. Don't be afraid to fail—see it as an opportunity to come that much closer to success as you grow and learn in your journey through life.

CHAPTER TWO

Your Internal Thoughts Change Your External World

Being a
Sacred Observer
Nurtures the Soul

As I sat at the United Airlines gate, I had to force my eyelids open just to keep from falling asleep. The annoyance of waiting, combined with the crankiness of being overly tired, was taking its toll. This would be my third flight in one day, and I still had an eight-hour trek ahead of me before I arrived back in the United States. I'd just finished an extended European speaking tour, and I was beyond ready to be home.

Boarding the plane, I dragged my carry-on luggage down the crowded aisle. I maneuvered past mothers with crying children and backpackers shoving huge bags into small overhead compartments. I kept checking row numbers as I searched for my seat—my own little oasis amidst the commotion. Even as I discovered that I had the middle seat, I sighed with relief upon arriving at my sanctuary—the place that would buffer my cramped body against the roar of the plane, the recycled air, and the canned music.

After my luggage was properly stowed and my coat and purse were tucked on the floor in front of me, I leaned back and settled in, ready to pass the hours as peacefully as possible. I casually fanned through the pages of the book I planned to read while the flight attendants covered the usual procedures. Glancing over at the man next to me, I noticed that he seemed stiff in his business suit. He stared blankly out the window and gave no sign of being aware of my presence. I imagined that he was attempting to avoid having to make conversation, but it seemed futile for him to go to such great lengths to remain aloof—I was feeling much too tired to take part in small talk anyway. I just closed my eyes and reminded myself that I'd be home before long.

Shortly thereafter, the man in the window seat pulled out a newspaper. As he opened it up and began to read, part of it fell into my lap. I'm normally a gracious woman; however, on airplanes, a sort of subpersonality emerges from my being, and I suddenly have well-defined personal "boundaries." I act as though there's an invisible wall between my seat and that of the person next to me, and woe be to the person who crosses that line! So I looked at the newspaper in my lap and gave the man my most disgruntled look. To my dismay, he was completely unfazed and simply continued reading. He made no effort to move the paper back into his own area.

With a number of hours left in the flight, I didn't want the sanctity of my "territory" impinged, so I quietly moved my hand under the pages on my lap, and with one swift motion, flipped them back in his direction. I wanted to give him an obvious hint to stay out of my space without having to verbally confront him.

Once again, as if completely unaware of his rudeness, the man casually turned another page, and the newspaper tumbled back into my lap. I looked around in shock, valiantly trying to find some reason to explain why this was happening. I noticed that this fellow's paper wasn't written in English, so I attempted to hypothesize that perhaps his cultural norms didn't include respecting the personal space of others—maybe he was ignorant about the unspoken barriers between seats on airplanes.

Resigning myself to the inevitable, I gingerly guided his paper back to his side each time he turned another page onto my lap. But after a while I internally started fuming, *Okay, this is war!* and began to shove the paper a little more forcefully toward his direction each time it encroached upon my space. *This is not a cultural problem—he just doesn't care! He's so self-absorbed that he thinks he doesn't need to pay attention to anyone else!* I became more enraged with every passing minute of his oblivion.

I searched my brain for some justification, and then it all became crystal clear to me: *I know why you're such a jerk. It's because I'm a woman. I bet you wouldn't do this to another man—oh, no! It's because I'm a woman that you think you can walk all over me!*

The thoughts just kept circulating inside of me and gathering more emotional charge as the man next to me blithely perused his paper: *Men can be so arrogant. They think that just because they're physically superior to women, they're superior in other ways, too. Well, buddy, I have news for you—this is one woman you can't walk all over!* All the signs seemed to point to his arrogance as I continued my internal dialogue of outrage with myself.

By this time, we were only an hour into the flight, and my silent fury had a long trip ahead. I was wondering how I could survive the long journey sitting next to a male-chauvinist pig, when the flight attendant announced over the loudspeaker: "Please feel free to get up and move around the cabin. For your safety, we ask that you keep your seat belt fastened while seated."

"The jerk," as I'd christened him in my mind, suddenly wadded up his paper, shoved it under his seat, and motioned that he'd like to get up. I had him! I impulsively decided not to get up to let him by—he could find his own way around me. While he struggled to get into the aisle, I thought, *Let's see how you like being squeezed!*

As he hurried toward the lavatories, I congratulated myself for giving the man what I thought he deserved. But when I looked back at him retreating awkwardly, I gasped in shock! The side of his body that had been against the window was mangled and deformed; and what's more, *he was missing his arm!* My jaw hung open as I tried to process this new piece of information.

Once it sunk in, I understood why the paper kept landing in my lap: He couldn't hold it with only one hand. I thought of all the built-up anger I'd harbored against this man and all the conclusions about his character that I'd made . . . none of which were probably true. The only truth was that some of the pages of his paper had fallen into my lap—I'd created all of the other negative details about him in order to explain his actions. I'd imagined a story in my mind about this man and had given meanings to his actions that had no bases in truth, and in the process, I'd dishonored him and disempowered myself.

As I watched him walk down the aisle, I was immediately reminded of another situation in which I'd falsely judged someone. After anxiously waiting in a long line for the ladies' room at an airport bathroom, I was eager for the next stall to become available. Finally, one in front of me opened, and a heavyset woman pushed past me, bombarding me with her strong perfume as she waddled by. I hurried into the stall hoping to escape her overpowering scent, only to find the toilet seat was covered with urine! As I scrubbed the rim with toilet paper, I ruminated about the woman's poor manners and thoughtlessness. I decided that if I saw her again in the airport, I was going to confront her about her self-centered rudeness.

Still fuming against the "toilet villain," I flushed and watched as a quantity of water shot up and onto the toilet seat. It hadn't been urine on the seat at all—it was water! As the true villain was revealed to me, I realized that the only offense of which the woman was guilty was wearing too much perfume. The person I'd proclaimed to be the enemy in that story I'd created in my mind was actually an innocent woman.

WHAT'S THE TRUTH?

It's not unusual to make up stories to explain the events in our lives. When something happens to us, we usually assign it meaning based upon our predetermined ideas about why things occur. We often try to understand what happens by applying what we already know about cause and effect—which can be useful, but can also lead to misunderstandings.

The experiences with the one-armed man and the erupting toilet made a deep impact on me. I thought of all the other times in my life when I'd made up stories and judgments about other people and situations. How much more peaceful my life would have been if I'd just asked myself, *What's true in this situation?* Instead of making negative assumptions about others and the situations I encounter, I'd save myself anguish if I could just become a "sacred observer" of what was true about the experience *without adding any of my own details to it.*

These days, when someone swerves in front of me in traffic, for instance, I remind myself that I don't know the whole story, instead of automatically deciding that that person is an inconsiderate idiot or an egomaniac. I recount what I know for sure is true, which is that a car swerved in front of me. I admit that I don't know (and may never know) why, and I resist the temptation to come up with a negative reason for taking it personally. I just notice what's happening and remain open to the possibility that there's a more harmonious explanation than the one I might create in my mind. By applying this thought process to everything that happens to me, I focus on just the facts and not on my assumptions.

At first it was difficult to be a sacred observer and not make presumptions, but it got easier each time I took a step back and reviewed what was true and what was a supposition. I found that I was better able to react calmly to people, and telling the truth about a situation ultimately nurtured my soul. Eventually, I gave up the notion that I could explain everything—I was finally able to just let things happen without judgment . . . nothing more, nothing less.

Of course it's human nature to judge what's in our environment; in fact, it's a survival technique. As we come into contact with the world around us, we often have to go further than observation and make judgments for our personal safety—this then helps us decide who to trust and who not to trust, as well as who's safe and who isn't. Yet so often we carry this very human trait too far, and it becomes detrimental to others as well as to ourselves.

Sitting next to the one-armed man on the airplane, I had spent an hour of my life in an unnecessary rage. My heartbeat and blood pressure rose, and my immune system was most likely diminished by the negative emotions that surged through my body . . . all of which because I chose to judge a situation rather than just be an observer. The truth was that a man's newspaper fell into my seat—*my* truth was that I was upset about my personal space being compromised. Everything else about the man and the situation I fabricated unnecessarily.

Similarly, the truth in the ladies' restroom was that the toilet seat was wet, and the origin of the moisture was unknown—*my* truth was that a wet toilet seat upset me. I could have just noticed the lid had fluid on it, wiped it off, and forgotten about it; instead, I spent unnecessary time and powerful emotions blaming the woman ahead of me. So by simply recounting the facts, without assumptions, I now have a strategy for reserving judgment and avoiding unnecessary strife.

STEPS TO EMPOWERMENT

As a beginning step, spend a day observing the way you react to people and situations. Remember that the instant that you judge someone, you lose the ability to influence them, so notice your thoughts and recognize if you're adding anything. Imagine that you could walk up to the person whose actions affect you and ask them directly if your assumptions are true. Is it possible that they could offer another explanation besides your own? The key is to ask yourself: *What's the truth? And what's my truth?* The answer to these two questions may not always be the same.

In every situation throughout the day, continually ask yourself these questions and notice what you've added to the observable truth. What meaning or judgments do you assign to the people and events you encounter? Are these meanings or judgments empowering or disempowering to you? Your soul loves the truth . . . so what *is* the truth?

Celebrate
the Successes
of Others

The rain soaked my hair as I stood on the London street, waiting for a taxicab to come into sight. The cold water slowly seeped through to my scalp, making my body shiver. *Why didn't I wear a hat?* I firmly rebuked myself as I tried to remember that the cabs coming toward me would be on my right. It didn't much matter, though—there were neither taxis nor cars of any kind coming from either direction, and there hadn't been for quite some time. I checked my watch again, even though I'd just looked at it seconds before. Everything seemed backward that morning, but time kept charging forward. Overhead, three wet crows circled aimlessly like tattered black rags blowing in the wind. They echoed the desperation I was feeling with every shrill caw they made.

I was on my way to Random House to meet with senior editors about publishing my books. Up until then, I'd only been carried by small publishing houses, so I really wanted to make a good impression . . . and being on time was of utmost importance. I'd never encountered any trouble hailing cabs in London before and couldn't figure out why it was taking so long on this particular day. I'd given myself plenty of time to get to the meeting, but I nevertheless feared that I'd be late if the situation didn't improve quickly. Cell phones didn't exist then, and there were no phone booths in sight—I began to feel helpless anxiety because I had no way to alert the publisher that I was running late.

Just then, I spied my taxi a few blocks down the road. I was suddenly rejuvenated as I glanced at my watch and realized that I could still make the meeting. I was waiting until the car got a bit closer before I hailed it when, seemingly out of nowhere, a man walked out, waved over *my* cab, and jumped right in!

How dare he take my cab? I saw it first—it was mine! Now I'll never make it on time! I despaired as bitterness began to boil inside of me. However, when I realized that my negative emotional state wasn't going to help me get a taxi, I stopped fuming. As I watched the black vehicle approach and imagined the man comfortably out of the rain and on the way to his destination, I reminded myself that it was important to celebrate the success of others (even when they had *my* cab), so I repeated silently, *I celebrate your success. I celebrate your success.*

The first few times I said it through gritted teeth—I didn't fully believe it. It was easy to celebrate the success of friends and family, but certainly not the good fortune of some stranger who'd nabbed my taxi. But over and over again, I kept chanting, "I celebrate your success," and it became a little easier each time I repeated it. Surprisingly, before I knew it, I truly felt a sense of support and joy for the unknown passenger. In fact, even though I didn't know him at all, I felt compassion for the man in the taxicab and rationalized that he might have needed it more than I did.

Then a miracle happened: The car came back and stopped in front of me, and a clean-shaven man, who looked to be about 40 years old and wearing an exquisite Italian suit, rolled down the window. With a wry smile and a penitent tone, he asked, "Would you like a ride?"—as if sharing cabs in London happened all the time.

His proposition took me by surprise at first, and I wondered if he had ulterior motives. I remembered all the warnings I'd been given as a child . . . especially never to get into cars with strangers. In a feeble attempt to stall my decision, I checked my watch again. A ferocious gust of wind pressed my wet clothes against my back and tossed my hair into my face. Pushing the strands out of my eyes in order to see, I slid into the car.

After we established that we'd go to my destination first, the driver headed toward Vauxhall Bridge Road in Pimlico. I let out a sigh of relief and began to relax. The man turned to me and asked in a slightly foreign accent if I chanted.

My eyes opened wide as I slowly nodded my head. Quietly he said, "I thought so," and turned to look out the window.

Although I found his question quite remarkable because I'd been doing just that when he stopped to pick me up, I was still a bit suspicious. My mind raced to identify the hidden reason that this man had asked his cab to stop for me: *Is he trying to pick me up? Is he hoping, even though he himself is well dressed, that I'll pay for the ride?*

I waited for his next move, but he just continued to look out the window and smile to himself, as if enjoying some unspoken secret. When we reached the Random House offices, I pulled out my wallet, but he waved me off firmly with his hand. "Please, allow me. It is my joy to provide this for you," he declared sweetly with a warm, knowing smile.

And with that gracious gesture, he quietly lowered his head as I stepped on the sidewalk and closed the car door. It wasn't until that moment that I looked down at my watch and realized that he'd gotten me to my destination exactly on time. I looked up to thank him, but the taxi had already departed . . . *in the opposite direction.*

As I stood on the sidewalk watching the taxi retrace its route, those powerful words echoed through my mind again: *Celebrate the success of others.*

There's Plenty to Go Around

In our culture we tend to think that there just isn't enough success, money, love, or good fortune to go around. For example, if a man wins the lottery, instead of celebrating with him, his friends will secretly wish that they'd won instead. Or if a fellow employee gets a promotion, instead of getting excited for her, her co-workers will think, *But what about me?*

We seem to believe the illusion that love, joy, beauty, prosperity, and peace exist only in limited amounts here on Earth, but the truth is that all of these things are abundantly available to any of us at any given time. The secret is that the more enthusiastic we are about *anyone's* triumphs, the more we'll glean victories in our own lives. What this means is that recognizing someone else's good fortune and being able to celebrate it—regardless of whether or not we know or even like them—has a direct connection to our own lives. It's often been said that what we focus on in life is what we reap.

Thus, it holds true that if you focus on success, then that's what you'll harvest. Directing your energy toward lack and limitation does only one thing for your life—it limits it.

Although it was a stretch for me in the beginning, I've come to believe that by celebrating the success of another—in this case, the unknown taxicab passenger—I received not only a free ride to my meeting, but I also learned an invaluable lesson about life along the way.

STEPS TO EMPOWERMENT

Whom do you know who's a success? If you can't think of anyone in your own life, then conjure up the image of some people in the public eye whom you deem successful. Make a list of these individuals, and after each person, write down all the reasons why he or she is so accomplished. These need not be huge triumphs—they can be as mundane as your gregarious neighbor who successfully organized a local community drive, or they can be as outstanding as Oprah Winfrey overcoming great personal obstacles to become the epitome of mainstream media success.

Then, one by one, rejoice in each achievement. For example, if your friend Mary was just asked to join the local theater troupe, you might write *Mary—great acting skills*. And then, either out loud or in your head, say something to the effect of, "It's great that Mary is such a fabulous actress. I'm thrilled that she made the troupe." Be sure to state it with conviction and with gusto because it's very important that you really mean what you say. Don't just mouth the words; truly feel enthusiastic about your friend's accomplishment. You may even want to top this off by sending a congratulatory card to her or offering to take her out to dinner.

Celebrating the success of others is especially important when a loved one, colleague, rival, or nemesis achieves something for which you yourself yearn. This can be a difficult exercise, but the

more you do it, the easier it becomes. This act of joy and celebra-
tion is one of life's secrets—practice it diligently, and the wonderful
things that occur in your own life will astound you.

EXPECT THE BEST

I stood by the side of the road with my thumb out, watching cars speed by without slowing down, while the wind whipped through my hair and tugged at my clothes. I didn't mind waiting for a ride because the view from where I stood looked out over the deep blue Adriatic Sea, and the sunlight shining on the water made jewellike sparkles dance on the surface. It was July 1969, and I was on summer break from college. I'd just attended a journalism conference in the former Yugoslavia and had some free time to travel before I had to head home. I wanted to "see the world," so I found myself hitchhiking alone in order to experience some of it. I thumbed my way through what is now Serbia, Bosnia and Herzegovina, Croatia, and Slovenia, and then I made my way to Italy and across to the south coast of France. In those days, it wasn't uncommon for a young woman to hitchhike alone in relatively safety. Although I also enjoyed traveling with companions, there was something exhilarating about doing it alone—I woke up every morning knowing that the day was going to be a wondrous adventure.

On this day, I'd almost given up on being picked up when two young and pudgy Italian brothers pulled over in their sports car and made room for me in their already cramped backseat. They were going toward Trieste, Italy, which was also my intended destination for the night. They were kind and adorable in an almost comical way—in fact, the way they both giggled when they talked reminded me of Tweedledee and Tweedledum from *Alice in Wonderland*.

The brothers' words of broken English spilled over each other as they excitedly explained what was bringing them to the city. They were from a small county village, but they were going to try their luck at gambling in the city casino. They'd been talking about the fact that they needed a good-luck charm for the night when they saw me on the side of the road with my thumb out. They were sure it was a sign from God and that they were meant to pick me up.

When we arrived in Trieste, the brothers were very honorable and graciously booked me into my own room in an elegant hotel—they weren't going to take any chances that something would happen to their luck. That evening they had me stand next to them at the gambling tables to improve their odds . . . as they lost money hand over fist. I felt that somehow it was my fault that they were losing; nevertheless, they were very sweet and said that they were sure they would have lost much more money if I hadn't been there. (After all, I was their "good-luck charm from God.") Since Venice was my next destination, they bought me a plastic gondola, which had tiny lights that glowed when you plugged it in, as a thank-you gift.

After I visited Venice, I hitchhiked through the rolling hills of Italy heading toward France. When my last ride dropped me off, I found myself on a particularly lovely stretch of Italian countryside. After walking for several hours without a single car passing me on the road, it didn't look like I'd get a ride before dark. So right after sunset, I strolled into a vineyard by the side of the road, unrolled my sleeping bag, and curled up beneath the old vines. (Whenever I couldn't get a ride into town or find a hostel, I enjoyed the solitude and fresh air that sleeping out under the stars provided. I'd already spent a number of wonderful nights sleeping outdoors under olive trees and along sandy stretches of beach.)

Settling into my sleeping bag, I looked up at the peaceful night. Silhouetted behind large bunches of not-quite-ripe grapes that hung above me was the expanse of the Milky Way. I drifted off to sleep easily with a smile on my face. Somewhere in the middle of the night, a barking dog awakened me . . . and I realized that it was barking at me! And right behind the dog was an elderly farmer with his flashlight pointed on my face, followed by his wife.

I smiled as broadly as I could, explaining to the farmer in sign language that I didn't have a place to stay for the night and that his vineyard seemed quite appealing. The man and his wife seemed to understand, and even courteously insisted that I spend the night in the spare room of their home. Their invitation was so sincere and kind that I gratefully accepted it. I followed them up to their 250-year-old stone cottage that was nestled on the side of a hill. The room that they gave me was simple—stone floor, stone walls, and a hand-hewn wooden bed—but I slept deeply and fully beneath the feather comforter. My last memory was of the stars framed by the stone opening that served as a window.

The next morning I was invited to eat breakfast with the old farmer and his wife on the terrace overlooking their vineyard. From the lofty perch, I could see down to the valley and even to the distant mountains. The couple seemed excited to have a visitor, and we communicated using a combination of hand signals and whatever words I could translate from my little guidebook. They served me fresh-squeezed orange juice with robust scrambled eggs, which came from the brightly colored chickens that scurried around the terrace.

With breakfast, they both drank a very potent cocktail that they'd made themselves from their grapes—and they were quite insistent that I imbibe with them. I put on a good show of tasting it, and they seemed very pleased that I "liked" their drink. Actually, the truth was that the beverage was so strong that it felt like it was peeling the skin off the inside of my mouth. But I didn't want to dishonor their hospitality, so I'd sip and pretend to swallow. Whenever they weren't looking, I'd quickly dump it into a plant . . . and they kept pouring my glass full every time it got low. (I still regret if I was the cause of that plant's early demise.)

Every time they poured more into my glass, they'd slap me on the shoulder, and we'd toast each other all over again. As I waved farewell after breakfast to continue on my journey, I left two very happy (and very drunk) people sitting on their terrace, proudly toasting me and gleefully waving good-bye.

You Attract What You Expect

On my hitchhiking journey through Europe, I was treated with kindness and generosity. From the Italian Tweedledee and Tweedledum brothers to the vineyard owners and the numerous other people I met on my journey, everyone I encountered was supportive and caring. During my adult life I've traveled to more than 30 countries, and I've always found the following to be true: No matter where I am, if I expect the best in others, I usually receive the best in response, even if that isn't the norm. For example, even though many people warned me before I traveled to France that the natives generally didn't like Americans, people in France have always treated me warmly. I believe that what one expects of people will manifest. Most of my life I've expected that people will be fair, generous, and kind . . . and for the most part, I've been treated with fairness, generosity, and kindness.

Some people have said, "Denise, you're incredibly naïve. How can you maintain this belief when a stranger, to whom you'd done nothing, shot you when you were 17 years old? Isn't it better to expect the worst in people and be pleasantly surprised when they aren't unkind, dishonest, or selfish?" I disagree with this sentiment.

Of course there are times to be wary of others and there are times to be on guard and to trust your intuition (especially regarding your own personal safety), but if you believe that shopkeepers will cheat you, then there's a higher possibility that they will. If you expect a car dealer to lie to you, then there's a greater chance that he will. *All negative behavior comes from fear.* The only reason that others will treat you poorly is because they're afraid that they have something to lose by not doing so. If you respond to someone with fear, then they're more likely to display bad behavior, and if you treat someone with love, they'll often respond in kind.

I believe that people are ultimately good and that if I treat others as I'd like to be treated, they'll care for me in the same way. This doesn't mean that I've never been cheated or lied to—it just means that I've decided to live my life expecting the best from people instead of being fearful and protective. I believe that this philosophy has brought wonderful people and experiences into my life.

When I was a child, my grandfather told me a story that illustrates this belief. A man is working in his garden when suddenly a stranger comes by and says, "I'm planning on moving to a new place. What are the people like in the town ahead?"

The gardener wipes his hands on his pants and poses a question of his own to the stranger, "What were the people like in your last town?"

"They were selfish cheats and liars," the stranger replies.

"Well, then, I'm sorry to tell you, but I think that you'll find that the people in this next town are dishonest swindlers as well."

"Thanks!" says the stranger, and he turns and walks in the opposite direction.

A little later, another person walks up to the gardener while he's kneeling over to pull up his turnips.

"Excuse me," interrupts the second man, "but I'm thinking of relocating to a new area, and I wonder what that town ahead is like?"

"What was your last town like?" asks the gardener.

"Oh, it was wonderful! The people who lived there were gentle and loving."

"Well," answers the gardener, "I think that you'll find very kind, loving people in the town ahead."

"Thanks!" says the stranger, as he walks toward town.

In my life, I've found that when I enter a situation expecting the worst, the worst is more likely to happen—but I've also recognized that I can still change my attitude midstream. For example, I bought a wheatgrass juicer from a local health-food store, and when I got it home and opened the box, I saw that it was broken.

I was hesitant to take it back to the shop because I'd never had a positive experience there, and everyone in the store always seemed grumpy. Since the juicer was very expensive, I decided to take it back anyway, even though I didn't expect that it would be a pleasant experience.

When I talked to the first store employee I encountered, she declared, "Oh, we never allow those to be returned. You can return anything else we sell here, but not that."

I knew it was going to be like this, I thought crankily and countered, "It was broken when I opened the box. If I'm not allowed to return it, even if it doesn't work, I should have been informed of that when I bought it."

"Well, I'm sorry that no one told you," she stated huffily, "but it's our policy—no returns on wheatgrass juicers."

I started to get mad, so she brought some other employees into the conversation, each of whom reiterated the policy that I couldn't return the juicer. Inside I seethed, *I knew it. These holier-than-tofu-types at this health-food store are always like this!* In short order, five angry employees surrounded me, and we were all arguing about the juicer.

Suddenly I had a realization—I'd come here on the defensive and had started my discourse by treating the employees as if they were already my enemies. I thought, *Wait a minute! I expected that they would treat me like this . . . and they are. I need to change my expectations.*

"Could I see the manager, please?" I inquired, but this time I changed gears and generated positive expectations for the conversation.

"He won't tell you anything that we aren't telling you," a saleswoman in a red tie-dyed shirt tersely replied.

"That's all right," I answered. "I'd like to see him anyway." I could feel a sense of relaxation and acceptance filling me as I thought about the good things I expected from this man.

When the manager came out, I explained the situation to him, but this time with the positive expectation that we were on the same team. After he listened to me, he smiled and said, "No problem at all. Sorry for the hassle," and he instantly refunded my money while all the other employees stood by with their mouths open. I realized that by changing my expectations, I'd transformed the outcome of the situation.

Now, changing your expectation doesn't always mean that you can change the circumstances of your life, but you'll be more likely to have positive experiences if you expect the best rather than anticipating the worst. Hence, if you find yourself in a circumstance where you aren't expecting the best, know that you *can* change direction midstream, and it may make all the difference.

STEPS TO EMPOWERMENT

Are there some situations in your life in which you don't expect the best? List these situations, and for the next ten days, think of ways that you can practice expecting the best. Before you head into a situation, take some time to examine your expectations, and if they seem at all negative, change them so that they reflect the positive things you'd like to see happen. Expect the best from waiters, salespeople, parking attendants, taxi drivers, co-workers, friends, family members, neighbors, strangers . . . everyone. The more you do this, the more often you'll see what you desire being displayed in others. If you expect even the meanest-spirited people to be loving and gracious, you may see them become that way right before your eyes. It can seem like a miracle, but it's within your own power to make it happen. And even if they don't change, it feels so much better to look for the good and expect the best in others rather than waiting for the sky to fall.

Proceed as If You've Already Achieved Your Goals

It was 7 P.M. sharp. I was nervous, so I checked my watch and checked it again less than a minute later—still 7 P.M. I looked up at the clock on the wall of the cavernous conference room I'd rented at the Sheraton in downtown Seattle. It said 7 P.M. as well.

I looked at the two chairs I'd placed side by side in the center of a room that could hold 400 people. The chairs faced the front of the room, and I stared back at them. They looked somewhat lonely . . . almost forlorn . . . so I dimmed the lights. They looked a little less depressing in the glow.

"Um, Denise?" a small voice from the doorway inquired. "Is this the right room?"

"This is it," I said. "I'm glad you made it. Here, let me take your coat, and go ahead and have a seat." I pointed to one of the two chairs.

Just then another woman stepped into the room. "Denise?" she asked.

"Yup, this is it. Come on in and have a seat," I said, indicating the other chair.

Both women sat in the chairs and looked at me a bit apprehensively. I quickly introduced them to one another and then walked to the front of the room. I stood in that huge room—empty except for two women sitting in the middle of it staring at me expectantly—and thought, *What in the hell am I doing here teaching a seminar for two people?*

Then I reminded myself that I was there because I was fulfilling a dream to teach courses for women. I'd gained so much on my own path as a woman that I wanted to share what I'd learned with others. It had been a dream in the back of my mind for a long time, and I'd finally decided to take action and make it a reality. I was trying the "act-as-if" method to achieve my goal.

I knew that one way to make one's secret yearnings a reality is to act as if they were true. I'd heard numerous stories of this technique working miracles for those who tried it. For example, I knew a woman who wished to increase her abundance, so she acted as if she were quite wealthy. Even though this lady had almost no money, she went to high-end car dealerships and test-drove expensive cars to decide which brand she preferred. She told herself that by doing so, she'd know what to buy when she finally could afford one. She also went into elegant restaurants and ordered a house salad or a cup of tea, over which she'd linger, figuring that this would enable her to gain the experience of being able to eat in such places whenever she wanted.

She confessed to me that most of her friends were horrified when they heard what she was doing. Well-meaning acquaintances told her that since she couldn't afford pricey cars or restaurants, pretending that she could was only going to make her feel worse about her situation. Yet despite her diminished economic status, this woman continued to act as if she were prosperous. Eventually she got a new job in a multilevel-marketing company that brought her some hefty commissions. In less than 18 months, she bought herself the Saab that she'd chosen from her test-drives and was regularly enjoying full-course meals at top eateries.

Remembering how well this act-as-if method had worked for my friend, I decided to use these same concepts to manifest my dream of successfully teaching seminars to women. So instead of planning my first one in my home or renting some space at the local library—which would have been a practical step—I wondered, *Where would a successful speaker give her training?* I immediately decided to rent a room at the downtown Sheraton for my first seminar.

It was a centrally located and beautifully designed hotel with rooms that could hold up to 400 people. Even though the rental was costly, I chose one of the largest meeting rooms because it was the kind that a successful seminar would have been held in. I could have hired a much smaller room—another practical step—but I didn't. I wanted to prove that I was serious about the success of this new venture in my life.

There's an expression in the Middle East that goes, "Trust in Allah, but tie up your camel." I take this to mean that even when you have faith that God will protect your camel, you still should take some action yourself to ensure that the camel doesn't run away. Needless to say, I failed to "tie up my camel" at the Sheraton. Although I exhibited my faith by renting a room, I hadn't taken action by sending out the brochures for the course far enough in advance for anyone to plan to attend. In fact, most people received the brochures *after* the event. I was still learning the act-as-if method, and I'd forgotten that after faith, there must be action.

I didn't actually have *anyone* enrolled for my first women's course—but since I'd already rented the space, I decided that I still needed to act as if I were conducting a fabulous seminar and asked two friends to come to my course as my guests. That's why I found myself standing at the front of an enormous meeting room with two pretend seminar attendees on one rainy Friday evening.

As I looked at their expectant faces, I felt a bit ridiculous. *Who am I kidding? This method doesn't work. I've just wasted a lot of money on this room, and I really don't have anything valuable to say anyway. We should just go out for dessert and call it a night,* I thought miserably as I looked into the hopeful eyes of my friends.

For the longest time I stared at them without saying anything. Then I cleared my throat a few times and fought back tears. I knew I was at a crossroads: I could either give up right then and there or I could act as if I were a seminar leader for women's courses.

Finally I took a huge breath and said, "I'd like to introduce myself and to give you a little bit of my background before I begin this seminar," and then I proceeded to give my talk. By the end of the evening, all of my previous tensions had melted away and I felt exhilarated. It had been an empowering experience, since my friends said that they really gained an immense amount of value from what I'd said. But most important, I now *felt* like a teacher of women's issues—my dream had become real!

Eight months later, through an amazing set of circumstances, I found myself giving another woman's seminar—this time it was in Australia, in front of more than 500 women. Within several months, I was traveling all over the world, leading women's workshops. (I eventually even wrote a book on the subject, called *Secrets & Mysteries: The Glory and Pleasure of Being a Woman*.) It's remarkable to remember when my dream actually did become real. It started with a small talk for two in a large room at a Seattle Sheraton . . . all because I'd been willing to act as if it were real.

ACT AS IF

Try this for yourself: If there's anything in your life that you truly desire, act as if it's already a reality. Believe with your whole heart that this will manifest, and proceed as if you already possess the qualities you yearn for. When you advance forward with the attitude that you've already attained your goals, it makes it ten times easier to achieve those goals. This is one of the secrets of manifesting your dreams.

One of the reasons that acting as if works is because it allows you to experience the *feeling* of your dream as reality—and once you have the feeling, you're halfway there. The important word here is *feeling,* and there are a number of things you can do to gain the sensation that the successful attainment of a goal will give you. One way is to use your body—for example, if you want to become more prosperous, imagine the feelings you'd have if you were. How would you walk and talk? What clothes would you wear? How would you carry yourself? (You might need to invest in an outfit that gives you the feeling of being abundant.)

Another method is to do some of the things you'd do if you were more successful. Perhaps go into a showroom that has the car that you'd drive and ask to test-drive it. Ask serious questions of the dealer, as if you were going to purchase the car. If you notice any limiting thoughts while you're testing out the vehicle, immediately douse them by telling yourself that it will be yours eventually. *Feel* what it would be like to really own and drive that car.

Perhaps what you desire is something more ethereal, such as inner peace. If this is the case, act as if you already had inner peace, noticing what you'd do differently. Instead of running from appointment to appointment, for instance, maybe you'd walk or drive more slowly. Or if you had inner peace, you'd wear different colors or breathe in a different way. Just a few days of carrying out this strategy can make an enormous difference. Acting as if can be the first step to manifesting the life of your dreams.

Then the second step is to take action. This means to decide what needs to be done to make your dream come true. Then create a plan of small but attainable steps that you can take to propel yourself in the direction of your dreams. Finally, schedule time to take those steps . . . and then keep your schedule. When you act as if *and* take action, almost anything is attainable.

Steps to Empowerment

Think of one dream that you have for yourself for the future. The first step is to write it out on a piece of paper with as much detail as you can. The next step is to spend some time visualizing exactly how you'd feel if that dream became a reality. Try to explore these feelings in as much depth as possible. The third step is to think of some ways that you could create that same feeling for yourself now. The final step is to take action—act as if this dream is already part of your reality. Start doing the things you listed as a means for your dream to come true. Imagine that you've already reached your goal. Always keep in mind that you'll soon attain it. If you consistently do these four steps, you'll find it much easier to make your dreams come true.

Where Your Intention Goes, Your Energy Flows

Try sitting for ten minutes and thinking about nothing—keep a completely blank mind. It's almost impossible, isn't it? Now try to think about nothing while contorting your legs into a painful position for hours—day after day—and asking yourself whether or not you feel enlightened. Does this sound more like torture? Does it strike you as crazy? It might be . . . but then again, it might not. I'd know—after all, I lived in a Zen Buddhist monastery where I did exactly that for more than two years of my life.

I was about 20 years old when I moved into the monastery (called a "zendo"). It seemed like a good idea at the time, for it was a respite from some of the challenges in my life that had led up to that point. And as difficult as the meditation was, it was also a very special time in my personal development.

Every morning I'd wake up at 4 A.M., before the sun had even contemplated rising for the day. I'd go to the meditation hall and sit on a small, hard pillow on the floor, facing the wall with my legs twisted into a lotus position. During the intense meditation periods known as *sesshins,* I'd sit like this for 16 hours without stopping . . . and I had to keep my spine ramrod straight while trying not to have any thoughts about anything.

From time to time, a Zen priest would come around with a *kyosaku stick,* and if he sensed that I was distracted by thoughts, he'd whack me on the shoulder. Even when it seemed that I *was* really focused, I'd still get hit with the kyosaku stick to spur me on. Either way, I got hit a lot. It might sound like a strange way to get enlightened, but Zen Buddhists have used this method for centuries. At the time, I also believed in the "no pain, no gain" philosophy of life, and since I was feeling so much pain, I was certain that I was well on the road to enlightenment.

There were times when I thought that I couldn't endure the severe back strain caused by sitting upright for so many hours, so I developed a special technique to survive the discomfort. I had to keep it a secret because our minds were supposed to be blank—we weren't allowed to visualize anything or to use our imagination while we were meditating. The *roshi* (Zen master) would have highly disapproved if he'd known what I was doing.

My method was simple: When the pain got very intense, I'd don a beatific expression so that the priest with the stick would think that I was in a *satori* (a spiritually blissful state), and I'd let my mind wander. I'd visualize the countries that I hoped to visit one day—although I'd traveled only sparingly, I'd enjoyed it and yearned to do more, so it was easy for me to imagine all the lands I desired to see.

The reason that this technique worked for me was because it's difficult for the mind to focus on two things at once. In other words, when I was totally immersed in my mental travel pictures, I didn't feel the pain in my back quite as much. As I imagined foreign lands, I also envisioned eating the local cuisine, meeting the indigenous peoples, and experiencing their traditions and customs. My visualizations became so real that at times I could actually smell the roasting coffee and taste the freshly baked bread in these exotic locales.

There was one place in particular that helped me through some of the more difficult sesshins, one where I could easily lose myself in vivid reverie. Sometimes hours would pass, and I wouldn't even realize it. In my mind, I'd see a small outdoor café in Italy, with red checkered tablecloths and the warm sun shining through overhead grapevines. It became so real that I could feel the sweetness of the grapes on my tongue as I bit into them. The sounds of the street echoed in my mind, while the intoxicating aromas of pizza and baking bread filled the air surrounding me. This place was a sanctuary in my mind that allowed me to survive the pain of the kyosaku stick and my stiff back.

When my two years in the monastery ended, I returned to normal life and no longer needed the escape my mental voyages had provided. It was as though all of the imaginary places that I'd mentally traveled to in my mind stayed in the monastery. It wasn't until years later that it all came flooding back to me.

I was sitting in a small café in the Italian countryside on a warm summer afternoon, sipping red wine and nibbling the most delicious crusty loaf, as the sun shimmered through the grapevines overhead. All of a sudden, I realized that I was in one of the locations that I'd visualized during my time at the zendo. It was exactly the same as I'd imagined it . . . it was as if the scene I'd mentally scripted had come to life!

This experience brought up all the other places and scenarios I'd so fervently visualized to survive my meditations. It was astonishing to discover that I'd not only realized my dream of travel, but the places that I'd conjured in my mind during my Zen meditations had manifested during my travels. I hadn't consciously tried to make it happen, yet it had all taken place effortlessly. It started when I was asked to give a lecture abroad, a number of years after leaving the calm, protected world of the zendo. Over the years, these invitations became more and more frequent until I was teaching and traveling around the world quite often—yet I never made the connection between my Zen meditations and the travel that I was doing. As I sat in that Italian café, however, I thought back to all the places that I'd been to since leaving the monastery (I'd taught in more than 20 countries and had toured many more). I realized that all the energy I put into my mental images of world travel had manifested in my life in a very powerful way. I'd actually visited every locale—and more—that I'd visualized while sitting sesshin.

SUCCESS CAN COME FROM FOCUSING
INTENTLY ON ONE THING

I believe that the intensity of my visualization for so many hours and days helped determine my destiny. Anything we focus on with enough determination has a good chance of coming to fruition. Unfortunately, most of us direct our attention toward things that don't empower us; instead, we focus on why we're unhappy or what we don't like about our bodies or our lives—and in return, this is what we manifest.

If we can turn our negative focus into a positive one, miracles can and do happen. An example of this occurred for my daughter, Meadow, when she was only about three years old. We'd recently moved to Seattle from California, and she didn't have any playmates in our new neighborhood, so she asked me why that was. She was very advanced verbally, even at the age of three, so it wasn't surprising to me that she was capable of such a mature, albeit heartbreaking, thought.

Not wanting to see my beautiful toddler so sad, I attempted to take the focus away from her lack of friends and told her that we were going to do a fun activity together. Drawing from the success that I knew had come from my visualizations in the zendo, I decided to try a similar technique with my daughter. We cut out photos from magazines that showed pictures of people hanging out together and pasted them into a collage. I told Meadow to imagine what it would be like to have companions, rather than worry about why she didn't have any at present. And while we did the activity, I talked to her about the power of visualization and affirmations—despite her youth, she appeared to understand.

Several days later, I heard strange whisperings coming from the living room. When I went to investigate, I found my little girl curled up on the couch, with her friend collage in hand, chanting over and over again: "A friend is coming to me. A friend is coming to me." (Although the way it sounded with her toddler pronunciation was more like, "A fwend es coming do me.")

Then the most remarkable thing happened. There was a knock on the door. When I opened it, to my great amazement, there was a girl about Meadow's age on my front porch with her mom, who said that she was looking for their missing dog. By coincidence, they'd just moved into the neighborhood, and it wasn't long before this little girl and my daughter became best pals. I believe that Meadow's belief, faith, and focused intent that a friend was coming to her helped her create the companion she desired.

Imagine what *you* could achieve if you spent time visualizing the things that would enrich your soul rather than focusing on what you didn't desire. Concentrating on these things can have a powerful and lasting impact, not only for yourself, but also for everyone around you and beyond. The human mind is an incredible—and often untapped or misused—tool for personal growth. A focused mind and heart have an immense power . . . together they can create magic!

STEPS TO EMPOWERMENT

If you're not happy with the circumstances of your life, change your focus. Keep in mind that you can always reach for a better, happier thought. Being able to shift your thinking is a powerful key to manifesting your dreams.

Is there anything negative in your world to which you're turning your attention? For example, are you always thinking about your need to lose weight, exercise more, work fewer hours, drink or smoke less, or do something else? Do you spend time every day focusing on how much weight you have to lose, how overworked you are, or how stressed you feel? If so, then you're actually contributing to being overweight, overworked, or stressed.

However, if you focus on how beautiful you already are and imagine how great you'd feel with a few less pounds, it becomes much easier to achieve your goal of weight loss. If you compliment yourself on the amount of work you *are* doing—and doing well—it becomes less of a chore and more of an achievement. If you quit worrying about stress and embrace it as an indicator of how involved in life you are, the pressure will lose its negativity and become more of a positive force for you.

Make a list of the negative aspects of your life on which you've focused your attention, and for each aspect, think of at least three ways that you can shift your attitude. For example, if you're always thinking about the fact that you feel stymied in your current job, imagine how it would feel to have a different one or even to work in a completely different field.

On the left side of your paper, you might write: *Stuck in my job.* Then next to this, you'd jot down all the ways that might change this situation, such as: *Find things about my job that are great* or *Quit this job and find one I love* or *Start my own business.* Now spend some time thinking about each situation and imagine how you'd feel in each instance. Which option feels the best? What does your soul really want? What would give you joy and happiness?

Once you have a clear idea of what you truly desire, start imagining this life for yourself. Focus your attention with all your might, and make it as real as you can in your mind. See it, smell it, and feel the sensations that come from living the life you've created for yourself. Gentle visualization isn't enough here—rather, you must imagine it with as much intensity and emotion as possible.

Return to this place often and continue to go deeper into the scene each time. As you do, release your attachment to your desired outcome, knowing that this or something better in accordance with your highest good is coming to you. This method of visualization has incredible power to lead you in the direction of the life you desire to live.

Ask Yourself
Empowering Questions

I was ready to give up—the high temperature had won. We'd been battling it all day, and I actually felt as if I were melting. As I glanced around the room, everyone else looked like they were melting, too. To say that it was unseasonably hot for late June in the Cascade Mountains would have been an understatement. I honestly think that our bodies were losing sweat faster than we could drink the gallons of iced tea we'd made. I was leading a residential seminar at the small cabin my husband, David, and I owned in an old coal-mining town in Washington State, but given the stifling weather, no one could focus on getting anything done. I had to think of something.

"Hey, everyone, put on your bathing suits, and grab a towel and some sunscreen. We're going swimming!" I hollered as I collected my things and headed for the door. Ten women whooped for joy, scrambled to get ready, and piled into my van.

Twelve miles from our house and up a winding mountain road was an alpine lake, which would be a perfect respite from the heat. The mountains were beautiful as we sailed past stately fir trees and through meadows splashed with color from vibrant wildflowers. As the paved road turned into a twisting dirt path and we continued our ascent, we began to see small clumps of snow in the shadows beneath the trees.

"Hey, look—snow!" someone shouted.

We looked out the window, amazed that despite the heat, there were still patches of snow that hadn't melted. The farther we climbed, the more the small clumps became bigger mounds of snow . . . until there were high banks on either side of the vehicle. *How could there be so much of it?* I wondered.

When the snow covered the road and got so deep and slippery that the van was beginning to slide, I announced, "This is where we stop," with as much bravado as I could muster. Since we'd come so far, it seemed a shame to go back without seeing the lake, so I pulled the van off to the side of the road and said, "The lake is just around the corner, so we can take a quick look at it before we turn around and go back. It doesn't look like we'll be swimming today."

Everyone was dressed in sandals, bathing suits, and straw hats, and we piled out of the van with our towels slung over our shoulders. Even though we hadn't brought any other clothes with us, it didn't matter. The air didn't feel very cold, and we were all game to walk the last stretch to the lake (which I'd assured them was very close). Sloshing through the snow, we walked around the bend . . . but there was no lake.

"Um, I'm sure it's around the *next* bend," I squeaked, praying that I was right. But it wasn't there either. Yet the miscalculations of the lake's location didn't seem to bother anyone—they were all in a joyous mood as they belted out songs and laughed in spite of the cold. I kept reassuring everyone that the lake was just around the next bend because I really thought it would be . . . but each time it wasn't. I was dismayed and silently chastised myself, *How could I have been so stupid to bring everyone here? Didn't I know that there would be snow? Why do I do such idiotic things?*

As we hiked up over the next knoll, we saw a truck spinning its wheels in the powder. Standing around it were several men and a woman dressed in high boots, woolen mittens, down vests, and knitted caps. Their mouths dropped open in amazement when they saw 11 women, ranging from their late 20s to mid-60s, marching over the hill in bathing suits and sandals. We must have looked like some kind of mirage to them.

"Looks like you guys need some help!" I shouted, as we all got behind the vehicle. To the astonishment of the stranded travelers, we pushed the truck right out of its rut. The ladies and I continued on our trek to the lake, while I continued to internally scold myself, *What was I thinking? I'm responsible for these women. Why don't I give these escapades a little forethought? Why am I always so impulsive?*

Eventually, we arrived at the lake . . . and it was spectacular, as the crystal clear water reflected the distant snow-capped mountains. Although tiny ice crystals were at the water's edge, the lake wasn't frozen, and a few of the gals even ventured in for a quick plunge. (After all, we *did* have on our bathing suits.) Once we were safely back at the van and heading downhill, I finally relaxed.

Later that evening, everyone agreed that it had been a great adventure, and members of the group thanked me for taking them on such an amazing trip. As I sat listening to their excitement, I realized that I hadn't experienced as much joy as everyone else due to the constant barrage of negative questions I kept inflicting upon myself. These bathing-suit-clad women had trusted me, and they'd experienced a glorious and carefree day—while I'd drowned myself in negativity. If I'd only known how the questions that we constantly ask ourselves can affect the way we feel, I could have experienced a greater depth of joy that day.

THE QUESTIONS WE ASK OURSELVES HOLD GREAT POWER

Every day we bombard ourselves with questions. Some are very simple, such as, *I wonder if I'll get to work on time?* or *Should I tell that man that his shoelace is untied?* Yet there are also recurring queries, such as, *Why does this always happen to me? What's wrong with me? Why can't I stop eating so much? Why can't I lose weight?* or *When will I ever learn?* These kinds of concerns are certainly not empowering.

Whenever you ask a question, your subconscious mind searches to find the answer, almost like a computer. For example, if you wonder, *Why do I always sabotage my relationships?* your subconscious will come up with a reply such as, "You have lousy relationships because that's all you deserve" or an equally nonproductive answer. If you inquire, *Why do I always overeat?* your subconscious will search for a response that fits the question, such as, "You eat too much because you have no discipline."

Your subconscious doesn't doubt the premise of your question—it just tries to find an answer. So whenever you ask yourself a negative question (or what I call an "unworthy question"), you'll get a negative answer, which will then just create more negativity in your life. Unworthy questions keep you in a victim mode, since they stand between you and the positive solution to your problem.

During my excursion to the alpine lake, for instance, instead of asking myself unworthy questions, I could have asked myself "noble questions" (as I now call them). For example, these might have included, *How can I create even more joy for myself and everyone with me right now?* or *What's the best way to make sure that the group is safe and has a great day?* At that point, my subconscious mind could have come up with creative solutions and I would have worried less, thus freeing myself to enjoy the experience more as we trekked through the summer snow.

STEPS TO EMPOWERMENT

Today, whenever you find yourself thinking an unworthy question, immediately replace it with an empowering, noble one. For example, if you find yourself thinking, *Why did this happen to me?* immediately replace it with a positive question, such as, *What value can I get out of this situation?* Noble questions can be better than affirmations because they lead to action—and once you're in action mode, you'll feel less the victim of a situation and more in control of your life.

You can also periodically create noble questions for yourself even when a situation doesn't demand it, such as, *How can I experience even more joy and love in my life right now?* Your mind doesn't doubt the premise that you're *already* experiencing joy and love; in fact, asking this question will only serve to help you respond with even more joy and love!

Your subconscious mind will also begin to search for answers to your question. For example, if you wonder, *How can I feel and be even more abundant?* your subconscious mind may come up with some innovative ideas for you to become more prosperous. Conversely, if you ask yourself, *Why don't I ever have any money?* your subconscious mind won't doubt your premise that you aren't prosperous. It may even give you an answer such as, "You don't have money because you don't work hard enough!" Make sure that your thoughts are always empowering, rather than disempowering.

Today, create one inspiring noble question to repeat over and over again. Some examples include: *How can I love and appreciate myself even more right now? How can I make a positive difference in the lives of those I love?* and *How can I radiate even greater health?*

GIVE YOUR BEST

On November 22, 1963, I was in the eighth grade and sitting in study hall, which was held in the school cafeteria. Suddenly, the crackling sound of the loudspeaker broke the strained silence. It was Mr. Brennan, the aging principal. The speaker popped with static as he cleared his voice. He usually only spoke to the entire school when he made lunchtime announcements, so it was strange to hear his voice in the middle of afternoon classes.

"Boys and girls," he started (he always called us "boys and girls" even though we were teenagers). "I have something very sad to announce—President Kennedy has been shot. We don't know any details other than that, but we'll let you know as soon as we do. I'm sorry."

The room was totally quiet. There were dozens of kids in it, but no one said a word. *It's a joke,* I thought irrationally. *The President hasn't been shot! They're pulling a joke on us.* And I started to laugh, shaking my head in disbelief. Laughter just snorted out of me, and it wasn't a tiny snigger—it was a huge, loud cackle. As soon as I started, the entire room erupted into hysterical, uproarious guffaws, and many students cracked up so much that tears ran down their cheeks.

The face of the teacher in charge of study hall went completely white, as she looked at us in shocked anger. She banged a book on a table, but no one responded—we just continued to laugh. "Be quiet! Now!" she roared.

Like a stone disappearing when it's dropped into a still pond, the room instantly became utterly quiet. When the teacher turned sharply and left the room, we tried not to look at each other. Some of us looked blankly out the window, while others sat quietly, trying to process what had happened. The teacher returned ten minutes later, and said in a low, solemn voice, "It's true. The President has been shot."

I couldn't believe it . . . and then it hit me all at once. Tears welled up in my eyes, but this time they weren't from laughter. I couldn't make them stop, and they splashed on the table and on my arms. All around me, other kids were crying, too. Not just the girls, but everyone—the "jocks," the "greasers," the "nerds"—shed tears. All the stupid categories that teens are usually divided into dissolved, and in that moment, we were united together in our shared grief. We all loved President Kennedy—he was young and vital, and he shone brightly with nobility and charisma. It just couldn't be true. He couldn't be dying . . . but he was.

When we received the news that he'd died from the gunshot wound, it felt as if something inside of me died that day as well. The President was more to me than a national figurehead—he'd become my idealized parent. In my eyes, President Kennedy was the benevolent authority figure that my parents hadn't been. I'd looked up to and admired him with all my heart. He was the hero that my father wasn't, nor would ever be. And now he was dead.

I grieved as if one of my own family members had died . . . and everyone I knew felt the same way. November 22, 1963 was a turning point for many of us, a date that we'd never forget. On that day, we lost our naïveté and watched our idyllic belief in the future begin to slip away. From that point on, our rose-tinted view of our governing leaders began to shrivel, and it would be only a few years later that we'd face the horrors of Vietnam head-on. But on that dark autumn day, all we knew was that our hero had been taken from us. And it seemed like everything radiant and shining perished with him.

After the President's death, I thought deeply about the challenge he'd given us in his inaugural address: "Ask not what your country can do for you—ask what you can do for your country." I took this sentence to heart, as if Mr. Kennedy had spoken it to me personally. These were words that I could live by.

Even though his image was later tarnished when information came out about his sexual proclivities and his political liaisons, I still never forgot the impact of the President saying, "Ask what you can do for your country." Over time, these words became even more personal, and I adapted them for my own use: "Ask not what life can give to you—ask what you can give to life." When I decided to follow this philosophy, I found that my greatest satisfaction came from making a contribution to others, rather than wondering what they could do for me. And the curious thing was that the more I gave from my heart, without expectations or hidden agendas, the more I received in return. And the reverse was true as well—anytime I looked to see what others could do for me, the more spiritual poverty I experienced.

HAPPINESS COMES THROUGH SERVICE

Although I continue to be sad about Kennedy's untimely death, his words still live on within me. They helped me develop the philosophy that if we want the best the world has to offer, we must give the world our best. Therefore, at the beginning of the day I often ask myself, *What can I contribute and give to life today?* When I do this, I find that my day becomes more fulfilling and my life feels more satisfying.

I believe that the way to happiness is through service to others. Whatever you give with a full heart comes back to you tenfold. It's important to remember that service to others is *not* the same as self-sacrifice. It doesn't mean that you don't take care of yourself first—it means that you share your life and energy without hesitation or conditions, and without needing to be appreciated. When you ask, *How can I serve? How can I contribute? What can I give?* you create a flow of energy. As that energy flows out of you into the universe, it also creates a great cycle that returns and flows back into you, bringing more energy with it along the way. But when you ask, *What about me? What do I get?* you actually stop or interrupt this life-affirming energy flow.

STEPS TO EMPOWERMENT

What can *you* do for life today? What's one thing that you can do to make a difference in someone else's life (or in your own)? Perhaps there's a random act of kindness that you can perform today. Maybe you could leave an uplifting message for the next person who uses your shopping cart, anonymously leave flowers at someone's doorstep, or clean up some roadside litter. It's a universal rule that the more you give from your heart, the more you will receive. Put another way, whatever you give, you will receive . . . tenfold. And the more you have, the more you can give.

CHAPTER THREE

Believe in Yourself . . . and Your Dreams Will Follow

Dream Big

Icradled the steaming cup of tea in my hands as I sat with my friend Ann. We were in the kitchen of her Capitol Hill home in Seattle, peering outside at the bleak January sky. There had been a snowstorm the week before, but now there were only patches of dirty snow dotting an otherwise muddy landscape.

"Want to go for a walk?" Ann chirped.

"Not really," I replied, wrapping my fingers around my mug to absorb its warmth. Even though I'd lived in Seattle for many years, I still wasn't accustomed to the gray dampness of winter. The city's cold dreariness invaded every part of my being and refused to let go until the cherry trees were in full bloom and the tulips had come and gone.

"Oh, come on!" she urged me, getting ready to go out. Out of obligation, I put on my coat and trailed after her, even as my internal reluctance lingered. While I trudged along, my friend skipped ahead. Then she whipped around and said, "I know—let's make a snow dragon!"

"What are you talking about? There's barely enough to even make a snow*ball* . . . and it's dirty," I said with disgust written all over my face.

"Don't you see, Denise? We're going to build a huge snow dragon right here!"

It couldn't have been more preposterous: We were standing on the side of a busy street with cars zooming by and muddied water being splashed everywhere. To make matters worse, the patches of snow around us were stained yellow and brown with what remained of the neighborhood dogs' territorial markings.

How can Ann even think that we could build a snow creature here . . . and why would we want to? I thought as I shivered and observed her bunch up a handful of snow to pack it into a ball.

While I stood by and watched, my friend rolled the snowball on the ground to increase its girth. She didn't seem to notice that it was lifting up big pieces of dog poop, but rather just kept rolling the snow into an increasingly larger ball. "Come on and help me!" she exclaimed.

I nodded, hardly believing that I was about to take part in this nonsense, and got down on the ground to help her push the growing snowball (all the while trying to avoid touching the yellow and brown parts). We rolled and rolled it, until finally Ann looked up at me and urgently exclaimed, "Denise, it's getting dark, but I can't stop. You've got to go back to the house and call the media! Get the TV and radio stations and the newspapers! Everyone's going to want to hear about this snow dragon!" she shouted with enthusiasm.

She's gone crazy, I thought. All I could see was a 20-inch, feces-covered ball of dirty snow.

"Hey, you know what? I've really gotta go home, Ann. It's getting late and I'm cold," I told her, feigning a smile over my shoulder as I walked away.

"Don't forget to call the newspapers!" she hollered back. I made some noncommittal sound, but I knew that I had no intention of calling anyone.

"Don't forget!" she yelled again, just as I was rounding the corner. The streetlights had flickered on, and as I looked back, I could see my friend working valiantly, scrambling to find more snow for her so-called masterpiece. I chuckled to myself—clearly, I was the sensible one.

I was drinking tea the following morning when the newspaper (which the paperboy always tossed more like a fastball than a printed document) hit the house with a loud thump. Still in my pajamas, I cracked open the door to get the paper, and glorious sunlight poured in. I remembered how dreadful the evening before had been and was much happier to sit in the sun than to roll snowballs in the cold. I unfolded *The Seattle Times* . . . and almost choked on my tea. On the front page was a big photo of Ann, standing next to a six-foot snow dragon.

It was beautiful—the tail gracefully curled around the body; and the long, thin neck supported a slightly ferocious-looking head. The article stated that a *Times* photographer had been on his way home from work when he saw Ann under the streetlight, putting the finishing touches on her snow dragon. Even though it was late (because she'd worked into the night), he'd grabbed his camera, taken the shot, and returned to the paper to get the story in.

I was dumbfounded. I'd never seen it coming—I'd had absolutely no faith in her crazy plan, but somehow my friend had believed in it and had made it happen.

REMEMBER THE SNOW DRAGON!

Ann hadn't made any calls to the media; nevertheless, she believed so fervently that her dragon was newsworthy that she wasn't at all surprised when the photographer came by. In fact, she'd probably assumed that I'd sent him!

You see, as we both looked at the ground of the same street corner, I'd seen only dirty snow while she'd seen the makings of a beautiful creature. To her, the dragon was already a reality—he was magnificent even before she'd molded the first handful of snow. I think that she believed in her dragon so much that her energy unfurled into the chilly night air and actually pulled the photographer to her. This is the way a powerful intention works . . . and I have Ann to thank for that lesson.

Now whenever someone tells me their dream—no matter how outlandish or improbable it may seem to me at the time—I remember Ann's snow dragon. I know that almost nothing is impossible if someone really believes in it. I also know now that my own dreams can come true if I can visualize them as a reality.

STEPS TO EMPOWERMENT

You've heard the expression "I'll believe it when I see it"—well, a truer statement is "I'll see it when I believe it." When you change the way you look at the world, the world around you changes . . . and dirty snow can become a glorious snow dragon. So what are your dreams? What do you really desire for the end of the day, the end of the week, the end of the month, and the end of the year? This is your opportunity to dream big and make these dreams a reality. Take this time to think about what you want and how you're going to attain it.

The secret to realizing your goals is to believe that you can absolutely have what you want. It doesn't do any good to wish for something and then tell yourself all the reasons why you can't have it or why it probably won't happen—this type of thinking limits your possibilities and diminishes your soul. Decide what you truly yearn for, and then don't just *think* it might be possible . . . *know* and *believe* with all your heart that it's inevitable.

Another powerful way of bringing your dreams to fruition is to act as though they've already been realized. Make a list of them, no matter how big or small they are, and then choose any one you want from the list. Next, write about it as if it's one year later and your dream has already been realized. If you want, you can write about it as though you're telling a friend in detail about the experience you've had or the feat you've accomplished.

This exercise can also be done *with* your friend. For example, if your dream is to get married, do more than just fantasize about the cake and the flowers at the wedding—describe it to her as if it's already taken place. Illustrate with words exactly how the scene looked, how the food smelled, how the champagne tasted, the look on your groom's face when he saw you walk down the aisle, and the way you felt when the two of you embraced. What was said in the toasts? Who danced with whom?

Now go beyond the wedding day and envision what happened in the year after the ceremony: What was the honeymoon like, and how did you celebrate your first anniversary? Create the life you want by dreaming it into existence. You'll be amazed at how easy it becomes to see the final dream manifest in your own life when you already believe that it exists. And remember, once you clearly see your dream, and you believe it with your whole heart . . . then take action to make it a reality.

Let Go of Judgments

When I was a young child, I loved to sing . . . but nobody else wanted to hear me.

"If you're going to wail like that, go outside," my father would say. And my mother would scold, "Denise, I told you not sing in the house!" I was shocked every time they said such things, because not only did I love to sing, but as far as I was concerned, I also sounded really good.

When it was time for me to enroll in the fourth grade, my brother Brand and I went to live with our grandparents out in California. (My mother had been committed to a mental hospital, and my father couldn't take care of four kids by himself, so we were divided among relatives.) On the first day of school, I was delighted to learn that everyone was required to take a music class that would teach us, among other things, how to sing. I loved the new songs we learned each week, and would often sing them to myself throughout the day just for the joy of it!

The first assembly of the year was to include a music recital, and our parents were invited to attend. Since mine were all the way in Ohio, my grandma and grandpa planned to attend instead.

Our class rehearsed diligently for the recital. I even practiced on my own sometimes in the morning as I showered, or in bed as I fell asleep at night. Before I knew it, the evening of the assembly had arrived. I put on a clean white shirt and black pants, as the music teacher had instructed us all to do, and brushed my hair until it seemed perfectly in place.

Later I stood on the school stage with the rest of my class. We could hear lots of busy chatter on the other side of the curtain, and I was nervous as we waited for it to open. Our teacher stood in front of us and said with a bright smile, "Now, everyone, before the curtain opens, just remember: All you need to do is sing your best."

Then she turned to look directly at me and continued, "And one more thing, Denise—your job is to just open and close your mouth. Pretend that you're singing, but don't let any sound come out."

I was so surprised that she'd singled me out for such embarrassing instructions, but before I could respond, the curtain burst open. I'd been so excited about singing the new songs for my grandparents, but as the music began to play for our opening song, "Oh! Susanna," I was on the verge of tears.

While everyone around me sang with enthusiasm, I stared blankly at the audience, noticing that all the parents were beaming. I could see my grandparents' faces overflowing with pride as they searched the chorus looking for their granddaughter, and I didn't know what to do. I looked at the other kids and was dismayed that no one seemed to care that the teacher had told me not to sing. I tried my best to move my mouth without making any noise, but it wasn't easy, and it certainly wasn't much fun. Then I decided to try to make up for it by pretending even more—I began to exaggerate my mouth movements and flurry my hands around for extra emphasis. It actually was kind of fun!

After the show, my grandparents didn't mention anything about my avant-garde performance; instead, they just kept saying how proud they were of me. Looking back, I can't say for sure whether they actually thought I was singing, or if they were just being kind because they didn't want to hurt my feelings.

The experience of the recital left its mark on me by contributing to a growing self-consciousness about my voice. I became afraid to sing in public, and my doubts and insecurities about my voice only got worse in my adult years. It wasn't until I was 33 years old that I attempted to overcome the negative feelings I'd developed about my voice by registering for a singing class.

There were 15 of us who showed up on the first day. We quietly waited 45 minutes for the teacher to arrive. Since I was already anxious about taking the class, having to sit awkwardly with a group of strangers only made things worse. *What if people laugh at me or talk about me after class? What if they feel sorry for me and try to hide their laughter? Or worst of all, what if my voice is so bad that the teacher thinks I'm hopeless and asks me to leave?* These thoughts raced through my mind as I tried to look calm.

When the teacher finally arrived, it was with an air of unabashed disregard for the fact that she'd kept us waiting. She plopped down in front of us as if it were a chore and asked someone to get her a cup of coffee. Clearly she had no intention of apologizing or getting to know our group—she just started telling us about what an accomplished singer she was and how many famous and important people she'd met throughout her career.

My patience was running thin. I'd come to improve my voice, and instead I was listening to this self-aggrandizing woman as she continued to stretch out her 15 minutes of fame. My mind grumbled with judgment, *Her hairstyle's out of date and her clothing style is tacky. Who does she think she's impressing with her tedious spiel? I can't believe the time and money I've wasted on this class!*

That's when the teacher stopped herself and announced to the group, "Don't let your judgments about me get in the way of getting results in this class." A floodlight went off in my mind—it was as if she were talking directly to me. I realized that before this woman could even begin to show me how to sing, my opinions about her had led me to conclude that I wasn't going to get anything out of the class. I was horrified to realize that my own thoughts were working against me.

It occurred to me that "punishing" her with my negative attitude—and subsequently not getting anything out of the class so I could be right about my opinions—wasn't going to affect her. She didn't care what I thought about her or if I got results from her class . . . *I* was the one who stood to lose if I didn't give it a shot. My failure would be my own fault because of *my* attitude, not because she'd been tardy or had overdone it with her introduction. With her simple, direct statement, my attitude reversed itself dramatically, and I decided that I was *not* going to let my judgments keep me from getting results! So even though my feelings about my instructor were there in the back of my mind, I resolved to move past my negative assumptions and gain as much as I could from the class. And the remarkable thing is that I really did.

I've come a long way since that day. Ten years later, I even found myself in a recording studio, sharing my spirit songs as part of a tape series. As I approached the microphone, I remembered with fondness the day when I chose to release my need to be right and embrace that carefree, song-filled little girl I once was.

DON'T LET YOUR JUDGMENTS STAND IN THE WAY OF GETTING RESULTS

It's human to make judgments—including the ones we make about ourselves as well as those we make about others. We do it all the time, and it's just part of being alive. It's easy to see how negative assessments about ourselves can have devastating effects, but it's also important to realize that *anytime we judge something or someone else in a negative way, we're also damaging ourselves.*

It's possible to make *observations* about people and situations without diminishing ourselves, but these are very different from judgments. In fact, observation is a kind of noticing without making *any* value judgment at all. For example, you can observe that someone appears to be homeless by looking at his clothing, his need for a shower, or the items he's lugging behind him on the street. Yet as soon as you move into thinking that he's dangerous, crazy, or dishonest simply because he doesn't have a home, you're making a judgment, and that can have a negative effect on your psyche.

Every time you make a negative assumption, you actually limit the joy available to you in the moment. And if you keep making the same ones over and over again, especially about yourself, you effectively become stuck in a place that denies you joy and positive growth. Before my realization in that singing class, for instance, my continual judgment about my voice grew increasingly negative over time, making it impossible for me to sing. I didn't do it alone, and I absolutely did not do it in front of anyone else—I was swimming in unconstructive feelings about my voice and cut off from something that potentially could have given me joy.

Similarly, being attached to negative assumptions about the world around you can cut you off from potential opportunities and friendships. Perhaps this has happened to you when you attended a gathering of new people. You might have immediately tried to discern which individuals you wanted to engage in conversation, and which ones you planned to avoid. Your arbitrary and instantaneous assumptions about people may have helped you establish wonderful new friendships and experiences, but if your view was narrow and judgmental, it may have also limited potential new acquaintances.

The best example I can give of this is the circumstance under which I met the woman who was destined to become one of my best friends. When I first met her, I was somewhat judgmental (and a little in awe of her) because of the way she looked. She was impeccably dressed, effortlessly poised in high-heeled boots, with flawless makeup and perfectly manicured nails. And her meticulously styled red hair bounced over her shoulders like an actress on *Charlie's Angels.*

She seemed so different from me in every way that I wasn't inclined to introduce myself. But then I remembered the words that I'd heard many years before in that singing class: *Don't let your judgments about me get in the way of results.* As soon as those words echoed in my mind, I realized that I was letting my negative judgments about this glamorous woman get in the way of introducing myself and getting to know her.

Because I was able to overthrow my negative assessments, we ended up connecting in a profound way. Had I been attached to my judgments, I would have missed out on knowing one of the best friends I've ever had. Later she was the one who flew across the country to be with me when I wasn't feeling particularly healthy. She spent a month at my house making me protein shakes, training with me at the gym, and boosting my morale just when I needed it most. When my mother passed away, this friend was the one who was truly there for me and comforted me with her compassion and humor. She was so much more than what I'd imagined her to be the first time I met her. I thank God that I was able to step beyond my preconceived notions to gain such a fabulous friendship.

Steps to Empowerment

Remember that when you negatively judge something or someone, you draw that negativity toward yourself as well. Whatever you focus on in your life will expand, so if you place your attention on what's great about your life, your success and fulfillment will grow. Yet if you continually focus on your problems, they'll grow in magnitude as well. Positive observations, judgments, and thoughts energize your life, while negative ones deplete your energy.

To experience the joy available to you in any moment, learn to observe—and not judge—yourself and the world around you with gentle humor. Think about the things, people, and situations that surround you, and ask yourself if it's really worth it to deny possible joy because of negative assessments about them.

On a piece of paper, write down three people, situations, or things about which you've made judgments, recently or in the past. It could be regarding a new co-worker, a friend of your child's, a particular location, or an idea. Consider each item on your list, one by one, and write the things that come to mind about each.

Next, identify which of these things are observations and which are judgments. An observation is what's true about a situation or a person, without adding a value assessment or a meaning to it. An example might be: *My co-worker eats lunch by herself.* A judgment, on the other hand, is an opinion of what you believe to be true about a situation or a person based on your experience with similar situations or people. An example might be: *My co-worker eats alone, so she must be egotistical—she must think that she's better than we are.*

If you've made only judgments, try to write out the observation that led you to the assumption you made. After you've done so, reread your observations and acknowledge that many of these things may by true, but also be open to the possibility that some of them could be inaccurate (or actually judgments). Go back to each judgment you wrote down and actively cross it out while you remind yourself that you're committed to seeing *past* these presumptions. And then, after each crossed-out judgment, write the observation.

In your future encounters with these people or situations, try to separate your observations from your judgments and remember your commitment. Make your thoughts more positive, and the outcome may surprise you . . . you may soon find yourself experiencing more joy and personal growth in your life.

Take Small Steps
to Make Your
Big Dreams Come True

I had a dream. I'd wanted it to become a reality for a long time, and it was always lurking in the recesses of my mind. I prayed that it would happen, and I visualized it over and over. Even though I sometimes doubted that it would ever materialize, I never gave up. You see, more than anything else in the whole world, I wanted to have my own place to conduct seminars. After years of traveling from country to country and continent to continent, giving workshops in all sorts of places—hotels, motels, and resorts; conference, business, and garden centers; churches, schools, and basements; restaurants, bookstores, and shops—I yearned for my own place.

Although I loved teaching around the globe, I was tired of being away from my family for such extended periods of time. I knew that it was difficult for David and Meadow to have me away so much, so if I had my own retreat center, I could spend less time on the road and more time at home with them.

I also felt that my seminars' attendees stood to gain a great deal from my having a home base. On the road, I generally held workshops for 200 to 400 participants at a time, and there were even instances where I found myself teaching as many as 1,000 people at once. Considering the short span of an evening lecture or even an all-day workshop and the number of people present, it was impossible to do any in-depth or one-on-one work.

While the energy created by the dynamic of hundreds of people in one room all focusing their attention on healing and self-growth was incredible, I believed that I could be even more effective by working with smaller groups for longer periods of time. I felt that in order to do this, I had to create my own retreat center. This would solve both of my dilemmas by bringing me closer to my seminar participants and allowing me to spend more time with my family.

I so yearned for this wish to come true that I spent hours visualizing what the place would look like, how I'd decorate it, and where it would be located. I prayed to the Creator and asked for guidance, and each morning I rose early and meditated on my dream. But despite all my efforts, time passed and I didn't seem any closer to making it a reality. David and I just couldn't afford it, so my goal kept getting put on the back burner . . . and I doubted if it would *ever* come to be.

One day, after years of visualizing, praying, and wishing, I realized that my dream wasn't impossible, but *my approach* was. I just needed to change my tactics. My retreat center didn't need to appear in perfect, completed form; it just needed to begin. I could start small and take little steps to reach my goal.

At that time, David and I owned a very modest, rustic cabin in an old mining town in the Cascade Mountains of Washington State. It wasn't much (the kitchen and dining room together were about 12' x 12' and not really big enough to run seminars), but I was determined to make it work. I figured that since there were two bedrooms, and one had a bunk bed from when Meadow was small, I'd be able to use the rooms to house a few participants. Of course that still left the considerable question of where to put the rest of the people, but no problem was too big for me to solve if I took one small step at a time.

I discovered that I could pitch six tents in the tiny backyard—they were all but touching each other—and these became the "rooms" of my retreat center. I bought two wooden picnic tables and placed them on the little bit of lawn that was left after the tents went up. We put an insta-carport-type tent over the picnic tables and called it "the dining room," and I found a friend who was willing to do the cooking. I bought loads of supplies (towels, sheets, and pots and pans) from the Salvation Army, Goodwill, and various discount stores in the area, and I was finally ready to start holding my own seminars. I'd created a retreat center! Although it looked more like a "tent city," it was my very own.

It was amazing . . . as soon as I began advertising, people started registering for my retreats. They came from all over the world—from Australia, Scandinavia, Africa, South America, China, Europe, and all across the United States—to stay in my tent city throughout the spring and summer. (It would have been too tough to sleep outside in the cold of winter, since the town was covered in as much as five feet of snow.) Even if it wasn't what I'd originally envisioned, I have many happy memories from the experience of leading retreats in my very own place. The participants gained value from the courses because I was able to do more one-on-one work with them, and at the end of the day, I was closer to my wonderful family.

By starting small, I was able to actually open the door to making my dream a reality. After a number of years of very successful and enjoyable retreats in the Cascades, David and I were eventually able to purchase a bigger place with ample space for retreats. We combined the money we'd saved with the sale of our tent-city property and family home in the city and purchased Summerhill Ranch in the Central Coast of California, where I still lead seminars today. And the most wonderful thing is that now I have the retreat center of my dreams!

Now that I'm finally living the "big dream" I'd visualized in the beginning, I know that the road to get there was paved by starting small. Big dreams are made up of little steps, yet no matter how minor they may have seemed at the time, they led me to where I am now . . . my wonderful retreat center at Summerhill Ranch.

THE POWER OF DREAMING SMALL

Wait a minute—aren't you supposed to dream *big?* Well, yes, it's good to have a larger vision of what you'd like in the future. But no matter how grand your dream is, don't make the mistake of feeling that it's so enormous that it's unattainable and will never happen . . . because that kind of thinking does nothing but push you further away from it.

If you've had a big desire for a long time and it's just not coming true—despite believing in it with all your might and acting as though it's not just a possibility but a reality—then I suggest that you change your tactics, just as I did. Start by dreaming small. This means that you need to start focusing on the steps, or "tiny dreams," that can lead to the big one. Be willing to make do with what you already have at your fingertips, and don't be afraid to get creative.

When I was young and just starting a family, for instance, David and I had very little money and barely any furniture. I dreamed of having furnishings that were fun, funky, and stylish, but we couldn't afford anything like that (especially since even scrounging the money together to buy groceries was a challenge at times). Then I opened my mind to the possibility of a smaller dream related to my larger vision.

A friend and I combed the alleys looking for things that people were throwing out, and we eventually found some old beat-up couches and chairs that we lugged home in David's pickup truck. We then painted cotton canvas from a local fabric store with latex house paint, making all sorts of artistic designs, and threw the canvas over the couches and chairs like slipcovers. Although it wasn't anything like department-store furniture, it did look pretty trendy—and I actually received a lot of compliments on my decor. If my friend and I hadn't been so creative and willing to try something "different," I might not have been happy with the furniture, or worse, might not have had furniture at all. The secret to dreaming small is not only to break what you want into small steps, but to also be willing to try a new angle—a different way of approaching it.

Also, keep in mind that a dream doesn't always happen overnight; that is, it takes time and nurturing, so don't get discouraged. Believe in your goal, and remember that the small steps you take each day are leading you toward it. In other words, if you plant an apple seed today, you can't expect to have ripe apples tomorrow—you'll need to continually water the plant and trust that it will bring you beautiful fruit. And so it is with your dreams . . . they're often reached when they're undertaken in bite-sized segments.

For example, if your dream is to go to Europe on a vacation, and you're no closer to doing so than you were ten years ago, it's time to dream small. Start by asking yourself: *What's the first step that would need to occur for this dream to come true?* Then determine what you'd need to do to have your wish come true. Maybe the first action you'd take would be to get your passport, plan your itinerary, or research hotels and choose the ones you like. Then work on attaining your next small goal. When enough minor dreams come true, your big wish will eventually become a reality.

Remember to also be creative and willing to look at your goal from a different angle. If going to Europe is currently far beyond your financial means, you could start by making reservations at a French or Spanish restaurant. Once there, imagine that you're actually dining in a picturesque European village. You could also go somewhere nearby that has a decidedly European feel to it, such as an English garden in the park, a Little Italy neighborhood, a French pastry store, or a local Scandinavian festival. Start soaking up the culture of your destination wherever you can find it, and begin experiencing the feelings you hope to get from a trip to Europe. These are all small steps connected to your larger goal, and they help to keep the dream alive.

Another area in which this method can work well is with weight loss. Have you been trying to lose 30 pounds for a long time and it just isn't happening? Do you tend to lose a couple of pounds but get down on yourself because you haven't lost more? Do you think, *What the heck—I'm never going to lose the weight,* start eating in frustration, and gain even more weight? Well, your big dream may be so large that it's getting in your way. It's time to dream small! Who says you have to lose all 30 pounds at once? Try taking little steps, and make your goal something like losing one pound at a time. Then celebrate like crazy when that one-pound dream comes true!

When you've successfully accomplished this several times, try another small dream by losing two pounds. Celebrate twice as much when you reach this goal. Creating small dreams and rejoicing every time you reach them will help you generate momentum on your journey toward your big dream.

STEPS TO EMPOWERMENT

Take some time to write down your big dreams and leave space under each one to list the necessary steps to achieve this goal. Chop it into small bits. What are things that you can do right now with the resources you have? What can you do today, tomorrow, next week, and next month that can make it start to feel more real? If you can, start to create a time line from these steps, setting a date for your dream to realistically come true. If you wrote down "one year," then list the steps that you need to take in order to reach the finish line within that time frame. Make small daily, weekly, and monthly goals for yourself—write them down and refer to them often, as they'll help you stick to your step-by-step plan. These are your small dreams, and don't forget to celebrate them as they come true!

With your list of the big dreams (and the smaller ones you'll aim for along the way), you're already one step closer to your goal—you've already accomplished one small step by doing this exercise, so congratulate yourself! Then keep going . . . choose another small dream on your list and take action. As soon as you accomplish it, celebrate your success as fully as if you'd accomplished your larger aim.

Success begets success, so be sure to let your subconscious know that you're in the game. Using this method, you'll be surprised by how fast you begin to check off your list of dreams, both big and small. Keep in mind that the time frame you set for yourself is just a guide, so don't be too attached to your dream coming true by that date—you might even be surprised to find that you reach it much sooner! Once you open the door and let the magic in, amazing miracles can happen along your journey of dreams.

Vote for Yourself

If you watch any television news channel, you'll undoubtedly see numerous stories relating to the inner workings of our government. That's because constitutional rights are a part of the conversation about so many of the topics that touch our lives.

While we may be tired of hearing about politics, there are some valuable life lessons that we can learn from them. Take the right to vote, for example. We hear time and time again that "every vote counts." We know that it's important to cast our votes for whomever or whatever we believe in, even though it's often hard to see the value of that one vote. And just as we can influence politics with our one vote, we have the power to influence our own lives with the way we "vote for ourselves." Let me explain how I know this to be true.

My daughter, Meadow, was in the fourth grade when her elementary school announced that elections would be held for student-council officers. Even though Meadow was younger than most of the other kids running for office, she felt that she'd make a good leader. Thus, she submitted her name as a candidate for school president.

When I asked my nine-year-old why she was running for office, she said that she thought she could make a difference. Even at a young age, she had a strong sense of purpose—but she also knew that it was going to be a tough battle. Election posters were plastered on the school hallways, and students quickly took advantage of opportunities to display catchy slogans. Posters for Julie Marks (who was running for school secretary), for instance, announced:

MARK YOUR BALLOT FOR MARKS. Meadow's name didn't lend itself to any snappy sayings, so she just put up posters that read MEADOW LINN FOR PRESIDENT.

The process was rich with lessons in integrity, fair play, and the workings of our political system. On the day of the election, the school printed ballots so that the students could authentically experience the democratic process of voting. When it came time for Meadow to cast her own vote, she was struck by an internal struggle she'd never considered before. She was a polite and gracious child who always thought of the needs of others before her own, so it occurred to her that maybe it wasn't nice for her to vote for herself.

I know that Tino is also a good candidate and would do a good job as president, so maybe I should vote for him, she thought as she stood there with her ballot and pencil in hand. But just as she was poised to mark Tino's name, she had another thought. *Maybe the right thing to do is vote for someone else, but I really want to win. I know I'll do a great job, but I don't know if it's right to vote for myself.*

Meadow later said that it was ethical agony arguing back and forth with herself, like having a devil on one of the shoulders and an angel on the other. She reasoned with herself for a while and then finally came to her conclusion: *I know I'll make an excellent president and will do the best job, so I have to vote for myself.* Despite her predicament of wondering whether her decision was the right moral one, Meadow checked the box for herself.

Later that afternoon, the ballots had been counted and the results were in. Meadow sat on the edge of her chair, as her teacher rose to announce the winners. She started by announcing the name of the person who'd won for secretary, then treasurer, and then vice president. It was agonizing to wait for the final results, but then the teacher finally said, "And your new school president is . . . Meadow Linn."

I won! I'm president! My daughter was incredulous as she received congratulations from her classmates, and she was surprised and overwhelmed with excitement. Later that day, the teacher took her aside, congratulated her on the win, and revealed something very surprising: "Meadow, I thought you might be interested to know that it was a very close race. You beat Tino by only one vote."

Wow, if I hadn't voted for myself, I wouldn't have won, Meadow realized. She told me later that the election had been a turning point for her, for she discovered that although it was good to be considerate of others, it was also immensely important to be one's own advocate. She realized that she had to believe in herself if she expected others to believe in her. This lesson certainly served her well throughout all areas of her entire life, not just the political ones.

CAST THE BALLOT FOR *YOU*

Sometimes the difference between winning and losing in life can be that one vote. It's particularly devastating when the one vote against you is the one you cast yourself. If you aren't your own advocate, who will be? You may find that you have opponents from time to time, but if *you* are also opposing yourself, you'll always be outnumbered. As a result, you might lose the election, job, relationship, or any other opportunity in which you might have made a contribution.

Although it's a good idea in general to be considerate of others and to acknowledge the qualities they may offer, it's vitally important to believe in your own attributes. When you're in the running for something that you really want, don't feel bad about admitting that you'd be great at it. Put aside your worry about others' feelings or how it will look—vote for yourself! It raises your self-esteem and energy level, and ultimately helps you win at whatever you're running for.

STEPS TO EMPOWERMENT

Where does *your* vote go? Are there areas in your life where you constantly put the needs of others before your own? Do you feel guilty "tooting your own horn"? Start by making a list of the areas where you don't vote for yourself and your own needs, or where you sabotage your desires in favor of others'. Then make a commitment to vote for yourself in these areas—determine a step that you could take today in one of these areas to begin serving and supporting yourself.

Are you willing to make a change? If not, ask yourself why. Try to come up with ways to start voting for yourself in these situations, rather than counting yourself out before you've even attempted to go for it. This is the first step in getting others to believe in you. And remember, every vote counts . . . especially your own.

Follow Your Passion

My first real introduction to the rituals of courting came as a result of my eighth-grade dances. These gatherings were held in the gymnasium of my school, which was located in a small Ohio farming town. On either side of the gym, chairs were lined up along the walls—girls sat on one side, boys were on the other, and parent and teacher chaperones mingled at the far end of the room. The lights were turned low, and when a slow song like "Moon River" came on over the speakers, the boys knew that it was their cue to get up and ask the girls to dance.

Upon hearing the first notes of the slow song, none of the guys would make a move until one very brave fellow would rise from his seat and walk stiffly toward the line of gals. Everyone's eyes would be on him—girls, boys, parents, and teachers—and when he finally reached the girls' side, he'd put out his hand to the gal of his choice. She'd either take his hand and dance with him or shake her head and reject him. If his hand was denied, he couldn't turn around and go back . . . he could never go back. This wasn't a formal rule, but everyone knew it nonetheless.

That boy had to ask another girl and hope that she wouldn't turn him down as well. His honor depended upon it! He'd keep going down the line of girls until someone accepted his offer. The catch-22 was that the more he was rejected, the harder it was for him to get a dance partner—girls didn't want to dance with someone who'd been turned down too many times. After a bit, a few more boys would walk the gauntlet, and by the end of the song, there would be a few couples dancing in the center of the gym while the rest of us watched and waited for the agony to be over.

When a popular rock-and-roll song played, however, the girls would be eager to move. Toes would be tapping and hands would mark the rhythm, but we couldn't get up and dance unless a boy came and asked us—those were the rules. Not all the boys felt comfortable dancing to the fast songs, so they sat on the sidelines. This meant that there were a lot of girls who desperately wanted to get out there but couldn't because they weren't asked.

A couple of times during the evening there would be a "turn-around dance." This meant that the girls could ask the boys, so we all could dance. As soon as they'd announce one of these, all of the girls would get in ready positions. We weren't allowed to get up from our chairs until the music started, but we'd brace our hands on the chairs, our bottoms barely touching the seats in preparation for the dash. The instant the first note played, we'd literally sprint across the floor in a mass-female surge. Sometimes two girls would ask the same boy to dance. One would shout, "He's mine!" grab the hapless guy by the wrist, and drag him off to the dance floor. I usually didn't have to deal with those head-to-head battles because I was a pretty good sprinter and usually got my first pick.

The turnaround dances were always slow. The problem I faced was that because I was taller than most of the boys, I never got to rest my head on my partner's shoulder while we danced. In fact, it wasn't uncommon for my partner to lean *his* head on *my* shoulder during a song.

At those school dances, all of the girls bounced along in their seats to songs by the Beach Boys or the Rolling Stones and desperately waited to be invited to dance. We hoped that someone—anyone—would ask us to dance so that we could get up and let loose. None of us had the courage to start dancing on our own without the boys. Looking back, I wish that I'd been brave enough to just go for it, but no girl had ever done this. It would have destroyed my "reputation" in less time than it would have taken me to walk from my chair to the middle of the dance floor. It just wasn't done. Girls didn't dance alone.

In a small Midwestern town at that time, we clung to our reputations like leeches holding on to their prey. Our reputations defined us and made us who we were. A girl who danced alone would have been called a show-off or a lesbian. Back in those days, anyone who didn't go along with the norm, even one in junior high, would have been accused of having Communist leanings. I guess we all reasoned that it just wasn't worth the risk to step beyond what was expected of us, even though it may have felt great to do so.

At that time, even though the rest of the country was in turmoil due to the Vietnam War, it was as if my small town had dropped out of time because the mores of the '50s continued to prevail, even through my high school years (from 1964 to 1968). During those four years, the inflexible rigors of dating etiquette prevailed, and no girl ever danced by herself at a school function. (When I was 17 years old, my town *did* label me a Communist anyway, but that's another story, which is recounted in my autobiography, *If I Can Forgive, So Can You*.)

LEAD THE PACK

It would be five years after my eighth-grade dances before I saw a female dancing alone in public. I'd just started college and was on my second beer at a party. All of a sudden someone threw on some music, and a hippie-looking girl with long straight hair and a colorful cotton tunic got right up and started going for it . . . all by herself! I could see people staring at her, and I even heard somebody on the sidelines say, "Show-off!" under her breath. But as I watched this girl dance, I could see that she didn't care what people thought. She took enormous pleasure in the rhythm of the music and in the way her body moved to the beat—her eyes were closed, and she seemed lost in her own reverie. I remember thinking that she'd probably danced alone at *her* school functions, and she probably hadn't cared what others thought then either.

I didn't have the courage to dance alone at that party—however, at the next one, I decided to try it. At first I was nervous, self-conscious, and worried about what others were thinking . . . but before I knew it, the beat of the music overtook me, and I just danced with joy. It was exhilarating! I disappeared into the sound, not caring what anyone thought or how I looked.

Later, when I thought about how much fun I'd had that night, I remembered all those school events where I'd sat on the sidelines, wishing that I could have had the courage to follow my heart and get up and dance. I'll bet there were a lot of girls at my school who would have also loved to dance on their own. If only one girl had gotten up first, I'm sure we all would have followed. We were all waiting for someone else to take the first step, and I regret that I wasn't the one to do it.

These days, when I find myself in situations where I have a choice between going the conventional route or experiencing joy, I remember what I learned in eighth grade—and I follow the path of joy regardless of the judgments of others. For example, I recently pulled into the parking lot of a shopping mall just as a huge rain-storm exploded. It was a bombastic downpour that thundered out of the sky like a jackhammer pounding the asphalt. Instead of waiting in my car for it to pass, I stepped out, raised my arms to the heavens, and danced a jig in the rain puddles. It was wonderful!

People running by holding newspapers over their heads glanced at me as if I were crazy, but I honestly didn't care—I was having too much fun. By the time I entered the store, I looked like I'd gone swimming in my clothes, but I felt exhilarated. I remembered all those years when I just sat back because I was afraid of what people would think of me . . . but now I don't intend to miss any more opportunities for joy in this life.

STEPS TO EMPOWERMENT

We often wait around to see if others are doing something before we feel all right about doing it ourselves. Why not be the individual who gives others permission? Why not be the first person to dance alone or run around in a rainstorm? Why not be the one who expresses joy in life regardless of the conventions of the time or place? Why wait for someone else to do it first so that you can follow?

Is there an area of your life where you're choosing to conform to the norm rather than the urgings of your heart because you're worried about what others might think? Are you living your life for others instead of for yourself? If you are, ask yourself these questions: *How long am I going to do it—one year? Two years? Forever? Is it worth it?*

It's not always easy to live life on your own terms. Adhering to the expectations of others is safer, but also far less rewarding. Yet living on your terms can begin with one step. Think of one thing that you want to do but have been afraid to try because of the potential judgments of others. Now what's a little thing that you could do today to chip away at this goal? For example, maybe you'd like to try in-line skating, but you're afraid that your family would tell you that you're too old for it, or it's too dangerous, or you'll make a fool of yourself. Maybe a small step would be to go to a shop that rents skates, try on a pair just to experience the way they feel, and then ask about lessons. It's a small step, but enough of them will get you to the top of a mountain.

Maybe you've fallen in love with someone who's substantially younger or older than you, but you think that your friends will judge you for being in this relationship. A small step might be to talk to your pals and tell them that you really like this person, and since their friendships are important to you, you'd appreciate their support in your relationship. They might not agree, but at least you've taken that small step in the direction of your happiness.

Don't be afraid to find your own ways of experiencing joy in life. Others may initially judge you, but most times they'll be doing so out of their own fears. Once they see how easy it is for you to choose to do what you makes you happy (even if it seems silly to them), and how much fun you're having doing it, they're bound to come along. Just think of those little eighth-grade girls who eventually followed some brave young spirit on to the dance floor. Think of how much fun they must have had boogying their little hearts away, and then blaze your own trail and see who follows.

CHAPTER FOUR

When in Doubt, Life Has a Way of Giving You a Sign

BE OPEN
TO MESSAGES

It was a typically quiet morning in our Green Lake neighborhood in Seattle. Mist was rising from the grass, and it was a little darker outside than usual because it was raining. I was standing over the stove scrambling eggs for breakfast when the cat door suddenly flung open and slammed shut with a loud snap, startling me. I swung around to see where Abby, our amber-colored kitty, was going—and I froze at what I saw on the cat door. *Oh my God, it's Jesus!* I thought, gasping in disbelief.

Since it was a rainy day, Abby must have been traipsing mud in and out of the house, and it had dried itself into an image of Jesus. It was all there—the kind eyes, the beard and mustache, and the flowing hair. It couldn't have been more accurate if someone had meticulously painted it . . . and he was looking straight at me! *Is this a sign?* I wondered. *Is Jesus trying to tell me something? Is he asking a question?*

I remembered reading about a woman in Texas who was cooking tortillas at her stove, and when she flipped one over, it looked liked Jesus Christ. When I saw the photo, I thought that it looked like a burned tortilla—nevertheless, thousands of individuals had made a pilgrimage to this woman's modest home in order to view the tortilla. A newspaper article recounted many miracles that people maintained had occurred after viewing it.

My initial thought was that I cherish my privacy and didn't want anyone coming to my house to look at my cat door. I told myself that it was only dirt and I should just clean it, yet I couldn't bring myself to wash off *Jesus,* especially when his eyes seemed to follow me around the kitchen . . . so I left it there.

My husband, David, had been gone for a few days, and when he returned, I showed him the cat door. "Yup, it sure looks like him," he said; "but maybe it's a young Jerry Garcia. Did you ever think of that?"

All right, I had to admit that it *did* also kind of resemble the late Grateful Dead guitarist, but I didn't want Deadheads flocking to my kitchen either. "Thanks—you're a lot of help!" I said.

David and I didn't talk about it again, so Christ stayed in our kitchen for months. I imagined that he was looking over my shoulder with a smile when I prepared meals for my family, and I even fantasized that he spoke to me at times.

This event occurred at a time in my life when I wondered if I was subconsciously being drawn toward Jesus—for example, around the same time, a crucifix mysteriously fell out of the air and landed at my feet. I found these events strange because I'd increasingly come to favor Buddhism and Taoism over Christianity. Too many wars had been fought and too many people had been tortured and murdered in that religion's name for me to adhere to the strict notion of being a Christian . . . yet there was Jesus Christ looking up at me every day.

As those soulful eyes watched me day after day, I began to think deeper about some of the ideals of Christianity. I considered the tenets of forgiveness, turning the other cheek, and treating others the way I wanted to be treated. These were ideals I could believe in, even if I couldn't hold fast to the actions of some Christians. My harsh judgments about Christianity began to melt away, as each morning I was greeted by Jesus at the cat door.

Not long after this, a neighbor threw some of his yard waste into our garden. At first I was incensed by his audacity, and my inclination was to do something to retaliate. Then I remembered Jesus on the cat door—and I realized that he was challenging me to be a better person. I repeated the Christian ideal of turning the other cheek to myself several times before I silently cleaned up the debris and forgot about it. It felt great not to be carting around resentment and anger concerning my neighbor's actions. I felt very fortunate to have recognized the sign on the cat door, and I vowed to continue to be open to future messages that might mysteriously materialize before me.

LOOK FOR SIGNS

Although most portents aren't as obvious as an image of Jesus, the universe is constantly communicating with you, whether you're conscious of it or not. You're receiving messages every day that can be carried on the wind, in the sound or the rhythm of ocean waves, or in the formations of the clouds you see out your window. They can come from ordinary events, as well as coincidences, synchronicities, and premonitions.

Communications from the realm of Spirit are delivered to you in many different ways. They can come in the conversations that you might overhear, the songs that play on the car radio, the billboards you notice, your nighttime dreams, and even in the random thoughts that float through your mind during your waking hours. If you're open to receiving these messages, you'll be able to learn from them, and you'll ultimately become more balanced and in harmony with the world around you simply because you're paying attention.

Often we can avoid difficult situations if we just take time to observe the signs in our surroundings . . . and this is one of the most important lessons that I've learned on my path. As I often mention in my lectures, and have recounted in the Preface to this book, it's powerful to remember that "if you don't listen to the whispers, you may have to hear the screams." What this means is that the signs all around us come first as slight nudges to help us on our way. It's when we fail to notice or respond to them that the messages can come with greater force, ranging from a brush with death to a minor fender bender or a bump on the head. The point is that Spirit will do whatever it needs to do to get our attention and give us the signs we need.

STEPS TO EMPOWERMENT

No matter where you are or what you're doing right now, stop. Take some time to look around and examine your environment, realizing that there are myriad signs surrounding you at this very moment. Notice the first thing that grabs your attention and ask yourself, *If there was a message for me from this object, what might it be?* And then imagine that you know the answer. It's important to use your imagination, for the keys to your inner realm dwell there.

Now look around again and notice the second thing that grabs your attention. Again, ask yourself the same question: *If there was a message for me in this object or event, what might it be?* And answer the question. Do this eight times, being aware of any kind of pattern in your answers. The recurring theme is your message for the moment.

~꒰ꔛ꒱~

Trust That
Your Path
Is Guided

"Just be back by sundown," my aunt called from the doorstep as I headed out to explore the desert with my knapsack filled with peanut-butter sandwiches and a thermos of water. And just like every other morning that summer, I hollered this over my shoulder as I skipped across the front lawn, "Don't worry, I'll be back before dinner!"

I was 11 years old and spending some time with my aunt and uncle in the Arizona desert. I treasured the hours alone each day, exploring the sagebrush-covered land. I was a child who always sought out wild places, no matter where I lived—I found immense solace in nature and often passed entire days out in the wilderness by myself.

My aunt seemed to understand my penchant for the outdoors, and as long as I was back by sunset, she paid little attention to where I went or for how long I was gone. However, she wasn't without concern for my safety, encouraging me to take stray dogs along on my walks for protection (there were always packs of them near the Indian reservation where she and my uncle lived). She explained that if I encountered a wild boar, the dogs would distract it long enough for me to escape, but reminded me that she didn't worry because she'd already prayed for my well-being.

I wasn't sure about the dog logic, but I always reassured her that I'd take one with me. However, although there were plenty of roving mutts in the area to follow me into the desert, they generally lost interest after a few hours and wandered back without me. I didn't have the heart to tell my aunt that I was usually out in the desert without the dogs.

I spent most of that particular day exploring. After hours of looking for lizards, following snake trails in the sand, and collecting prickly pears, it was late afternoon when I arrived at the base of a high mesa. My dog companions had long since headed for home, but I didn't give much thought to the dangers of being alone. In all the weeks that I'd been there, I had yet to see a wild boar. I was pretty sure that my aunt had been exaggerating. Fearlessly sizing up the climb ahead of me, I estimated that I could reach the top in time for a sunset that was promising to be spectacular because of the gathering clouds along the western horizon.

The mesa wall was more challenging to climb than I'd anticipated. Loose rocks and shale slid beneath my feet, and I knew that one slip could send me tumbling into the long, spiny thorns of a nearby cactus. Consequently, I maintained a very slow and deliberate pace, looking carefully before each step so as to avoid a fall.

It took several arduous hours to reach the mesa top, but once I did, it was well worth the journey. The sunset splashed across the entire sky with brilliant shades of orange, red, and deep purple. Mesmerized by its ever-changing colors, I couldn't pull my eyes away until the last streak of red faded and the stars began to take their places in the sky. All at once, like a curtain closing at the end of a play, I found myself sitting in the dark auditorium of night.

Suddenly I felt small compared to the infinite space around me. I'd completely lost track of time. Somehow it never occurred to me that watching the sunset meant that I'd be walking back after dark. The trek was going to be a hard one—in addition, it would take significantly longer at night. I began by taking delicate steps down the dangerous decline, hoping to avoid any cactus spines.

I tried to remain calm as I imagined my aunt and uncle worrying at home, but after 20 minutes of struggling to get down the mesa wall, tears soaked my cheeks. I kept sliding down the rocky slope, and my aunt and uncle's house felt like it was a million miles away. I was telling myself to be more careful when I abruptly slipped on a rock and my feet flew out from under me. Momentarily airborne, I sailed down the hill a few yards before crashing to the ground. I wasn't hurt, but I continued to lie there for a few seconds looking up at the stars . . . and then the strangest thing happened.

My aunt spontaneously appeared in my mind—her image was so vivid and real. While I considered her a very spiritual person, especially in light of the fact that both of my parents were atheists, I didn't consider *myself* that spiritual. At 11 years of age, I still wasn't sure whether or not God even existed, yet at that moment, as she serenely gazed into my eyes, I felt calm and comforted, as if her arms were wrapping around me to help me to my feet. I could hear my aunt's voice saying that she never worried about me because she'd already prayed for God to protect me, and it was almost as if she were saying that I could do the same for myself—all I had to do was ask for help if I needed it. So, despite the fact that I'd never done so before, I prayed in a soft whisper, "God, please help me make it home safely."

THE PROTECTION OF THE INVISIBLE REALM

Back on my feet, I started down the mesa again, but remarkably my steps now felt light and full of energy, as though my every move were being guided—I even found it hard to keep a smile off my face. Although it was extremely precarious going downhill in complete darkness, I floated along almost effortlessly and reached the bottom in far less time than it had taken me to ascend in broad daylight. Somehow, on a moonless night . . . in treacherous desert terrain . . . with a wild boar possibly lurking nearby, I swiftly and safely made my way back to my aunt and uncle's home as if I had wings.

Both of them were pacing in the living room and on the verge of calling the police when I burst through the front door with joyful exuberance. I apologized, and promised never to come back so late again. I later told my aunt that I'd stayed on the mesa to watch the sunset and had walked back in the dark. She said that it was a miracle I hadn't been hurt on the descent. I silently agreed to myself that it had indeed been a miracle. I thought back to how effortlessly I'd descended the cliff and found my way home. I knew for certain that my prayer had worked, and invisible helpers had guided me along the way.

Although I couldn't fully articulate it at that moment, I've come to understand that what I was experiencing was the existence of an invisible realm. Some things are true whether or not you believe them, and I now know that there are loving beings that always watch over and care for us. And when we ask them to, they guide us where we need to go.

STEPS TO EMPOWERMENT

To connect with your invisible helpers and ask them to aid you through difficult situations, close your eyes and take a few moments to be completely still. Allow yourself to move deeply into the center of your being. (Since this is a sacred and quiet place within you, it's important that you take as much time as you need to reach it.) When you're ready, breathe deeply. As you exhale, say, "To the Creator that dwells within all things, I ask for guidance and blessings, and I send peace. Thank You." Continue to softly repeat these words several times while you imagine a feeling of peace and tranquility filling your heart. Trust that assistance is on the way.

You can return to this exercise whenever you feel the need. Additionally, you can ask in your own words, for it isn't what you say that matters, it's what's in your heart. If you feel that all you want to say is "Help!" then go with it. As you focus on your message, have faith that it will be heard, and know that assistance is on the way. Trust that invisible forces dedicated to your well-being surround you at all times. You can harness their strength and guidance whenever you need them. They're only a thought away . . . it's simply a matter of asking for help.

Every Prayer
Is Heard

Imagine for a moment that you've just jumped off the edge of a boat into a brisk mountain lake or a sparkling tropical ocean. You've plunged beneath the surface and your whole body is submerged—you can feel the presence of water everywhere, surrounding you in all directions. Now consider the invisible domain of the spirit world and visualize that it surrounds you (and everyone else) in much the same way. It's present at all times and fills in all areas of the space around you, just like water does. It can touch you as profoundly as a snow-fed mountain lake engulfs your body as you dive into its crystal clear depths.

I'm aware of this realm because I've experienced it numerous times throughout my life. It can seem scary or confusing, exciting or enlightening, but it's always mysterious and wondrous for me. There was one experience in particular that has always stayed with me. It happened many years ago while I was spending two weeks in Indonesia.

I was with my husband and daughter on the island nation of Bali, leading a healing retreat seminar. Bali is a very powerful place for me—it radiates a palpable mystical energy, and unexplainable experiences abound there. I have the sense that it's been that way for centuries, or maybe even longer. As a child, I remember my mother telling me stories about the magical things that happened in that tropical land. (She and her first husband, a native of the neighboring island of Java, had lived on a Balinese plantation that was owned by his family.) Being there and seeing the lush landscape for myself, after having heard so many amazing stories as a kid, was a remarkable experience.

At my retreat, I was teaching about a healing system that I'd developed, and I was especially proud of the title I'd given to the program. Calling it "The White Owl Seminar," it seemed to speak to the parallels between an owl, which uses its senses to navigate accurately through the dark night, and a spiritual healer, who needs to sense energies that can't always be seen.

I was leading a large group, about 100 participants in all, and I had a staff of 12 assistants working with me. On the morning of a particularly important segment of the retreat, I called the assistants together to make plans to meet with them during the lunch break. We all checked our watches to make sure that we were synchronized, and we agreed upon a meeting place. At 1 P.M. exactly, I arrived at our designated spot and was surprised to find only half of the group there. Unsure of what to do, we had our discussion and returned to the seminar. When we got there, the missing half of the group came storming toward us, wondering where we'd been and why we'd called a meeting if we weren't going to show up.

"Hey," I retorted, "I was just going to ask you guys the same question!"

How could it be that we were all sure that we'd been in the same place at the same time, yet we'd missed each other? When I later gathered everybody together to discuss what had happened, we all rechecked our watches and verified that we'd all had the right meeting spot in mind. Everyone concluded that we'd indeed all been at the same place at the same time, yet something very strange had happened—it was as if a time loop had kept us apart. I couldn't explain why it had happened, but it seemed to be an affirmation of the invisible realm that operated outside of the space-time continuum. We'd somehow passed right through it!

On that same trip, I had another brush with the invisible realm and the spiritual beings that inhabit it. I was already feeling aware of the fact that in Bali, the line between ordinary, everyday life and the realm of Spirit was teetering somewhere between thin and nonexistent. I sometimes felt as if it was hard to tell where one reality ended and the other began.

The seminar had wrapped up, and the bus driver was loading the last of the suitcases into the storage compartment. I was feeling uncertain about the success of the program and uneasy about whether or not the participants would be able to use what they'd learned there in their own day-to-day lives. I walked down to the nearby beach one last time before leaving to think about it.

As I rolled up my pants and stood knee-deep in the surf, the force of the water rushing back out to sea tugged at me and made it difficult to keep standing in one place. Nevertheless, I enjoyed the coolness of the water on my legs and the refreshing, salty taste in the air. As white foam danced powerfully around me, I decided to talk to the Creator and ask for some guidance. I began by looking across the ocean as far as I could, and then I turned back around to watch the palm trees sway along the sandy shore. I felt immense gratitude for my time in Bali, and I was so thankful for the wonderful experience of the seminar and for having my family there with me.

Smiling and turning my eyes upward (as I'm accustomed to doing when I speak to the Creator, even though I don't believe She's "up there," per se), I slowly began my plea, *God, I need Your help. It seems that remarkable things happened for people during this seminar, but right now I wonder if it's really going to make a difference in their lives. How can I know if this was a valuable experience for my students?*

As I stood in the surf with my head tilted toward the sky, beseeching the heavens to give me some sort of concrete sign, I considered the possibility that my efforts might have been in vain. Was I praying to something that I just made up or imagined? Despite previous signs from the spirit realm and life-changing events such as the near-death experience I had at age 17, I still had moments when I doubted the existence of God. Sometimes I'd even laugh off the idea of guardian angels because I'd get so caught up in the physical world that the spiritual one would slowly fall away, until it felt like something I'd dreamed about once.

Having finished my prayer, I started to feel a little self-conscious about just standing there and staring at the sky, so I decided to head back toward the bus. Just as I was about to make my way out of the water, I felt something heavy and hard bump up against my leg. I rummaged around in the surf to see if I could grab it—my fingers grasped something solid and smooth, and I curiously pulled it out of the water. I was rendered speechless by what I saw in the palm of my hand. It was a piece of white quartz crystal *carved in the perfect shape of an owl!* I just stared at it, blinking in astonishment. My question had been answered, and I was sure that my students *would* get results from their participation. I hadn't prayed in vain—I had been heard.

I've always kept that quartz owl as a reminder to myself that the spiritual realm hears our pleas . . . even when we don't believe it.

WE ONLY NEED TO ASK . . .

Although we have different names for the Divine Source—God, Goddess, Spirit, Guardian Angel, Great Spirit, Creator—it's undeniable that a very real, although invisible, spiritual power exists around us at all times. And it's not just for a few people—it's for everyone. Each one of us can call upon this realm when we need guidance. Think of our access to it like our access to the sun. The sun isn't only for certain individuals or for those who are privileged—it exists for all beings. All we have to do is to step out of the shadows into the light.

It helps to think of the invisible realm in the same way we think of the sun. We might not be able to explain exactly what it's made of or precisely how we came to inhabit an earth that orbits it, but we can feel its warmth and see its light, and we're affected by its power. Anyone who's willing to walk outside on a sunny day can experience its glorious rays—just as the Creator and the beings of the spiritual realm are available to anyone who's willing to receive them. All we need do is ask.

STEPS TO EMPOWERMENT

Whether you're standing on a beach in Bali or in the backyard of your own barrio, there's a spiritual world that surrounds you and has the power to guide your life, even if you aren't always sure that it exists. You *do* have personal spirit guardians that listen to you, care for you, and will respond to you when you reach out to them. It's simply a matter of taking that plunge, basking in that sunshine, asking for that guidance from the spiritual realm . . . and most important, being open to hearing their answers.

As an exercise, find a peaceful place where you feel at home—it might be in a secluded section of a park, with your back against a tree on your yard, or a corner of your living room. Then, to help you connect with the invisible presence within and around you, close your eyes and take a few moments to be still. (Be patient and try not to rush this aspect of your exercise.) Once you're calm and centered, take a few moments to focus on the things that you're thankful for. Think about the aspects of, or the people in, your life that you're grateful for: your friends and family, the blessings you've received in your career, your possessions, or your physical body. Let the feeling of thankfulness envelop you until you feel completely saturated with appreciation.

Now ask your heartfelt questions and make your plea for guidance. You don't need to use eloquent words, just use ones that feel like they come straight from your soul. I like to add this short phrase at the end of my requests that may prove helpful for you as well: "in accordance with my highest good." For example, if your prayer is to receive a passing grade on an exam, you might pray, "Please, Divine Source, I ask for Your help in receiving a passing grade, in accordance with my highest good." Adding this phrase reinforces that you're open to receiving answers that align with your greatest potential and your deepest spiritual good.

Always be patient with your prayers. Know that while the answers might come in their own way and at their own time, each prayer is *always* heard by the spiritual realm.

⌘

THE CREATOR
IS EVERYWHERE

When I was younger, I never wanted to go to hospitals or see doctors of any kind . . . ever! As a result of some negative experiences with the medical field, I became a fierce advocate of "natural health." In fact, I was so adamant about my position that I opted to give birth to my daughter at home, even though there was a possibility that I might not survive the delivery. As a teenage victim of a random act of violence, my body had suffered severe permanent injuries from gunshot wounds, and I'd been warned that if complications had arisen from this incident, having the baby at home could prove deadly.

Fortunately, my daughter's delivery was safe and relatively easy. The second time I was pregnant, however, I was not so fortunate. A number of years after Meadow was born, I was in the third month of my pregnancy when I suddenly began to experience excruciating cramps and bleeding. I was alone in the kitchen when I realized what was happening to me. My husband, David, was working late, and although I tried to call him at work several times, I couldn't get through.

Trying to remain calm enough to figure out what to do, I prayed that I could find the strength to handle the situation by myself. Our family didn't have medical insurance, and since we had little money, I didn't want to call for an ambulance that I knew would be very expensive. So I decided to ride it out in the bathroom.

Sitting on the toilet, I was on the verge of panic when the blood started to gush from my body. *The baby! What about the baby? I can't have it go down the toilet,* I thought frantically. While I knew that the fetus would be no bigger than a kidney bean, I still thought of it as my child. I climbed into the bathtub, plugged the drain, and determinedly decided, *My baby is not going down the drain!*

As my blood flowed into the bathtub, I kept running my hands through it, looking for the fetus. *Where is it? What if I can't find it?* Finally I found a little bean-shaped object that could have been a clot, but I was sure that it was my baby. Sobbing uncontrollably, I stroked the small object and mumbled through tears, "I'm so sorry . . . I'm so sorry."

I sat in the bathtub, engulfed by guilt, and realized that I was starting to feel very cold and dizzy. Somewhere inside of me, a voice said, *You are losing too much blood. You need to get help.* When I looked around, I became aware that the walls looked blurry and out of focus—by then, the inner voice was shouting at me with a sense of urgency, *You need to get help! Get up!*

I mustered the strength to get out of the bathtub, wrapped myself in a towel, and placed my little bean-shaped baby in an empty soap dish. As I stumbled to the kitchen, holding the dish, I prayed that I wouldn't pass out before I could get to the phone.

Before I could call for help, however, I had to make sure that nothing happened to the baby I was carrying in the soap dish. Once it was safely in the refrigerator, I reached for the phone, while fresh blood dripped onto the kitchen floor, and dialed my neighbor. "I'm having a miscarriage," was all I could utter before I dropped the phone. By the time she arrived, I could barely hold myself up.

"We have to get you to the hospital!" she exclaimed without another thought.

"I don't want to go to the hospital."

"Denise, you have to! This is serious." She looked like she was about to cry.

Suddenly, I heard the voice inside of me speak again, *Denise, God dwells in hospitals, too.*

Normally, I would have done anything to avoid a hospital. Yet a calm feeling came over me as those words echoed in my mind. "You're right," I told my friend. "Everything will be okay. I'm ready to go now."

At the emergency room, doctors stopped the bleeding and assured me that although I'd lost a considerable amount of blood, I was going to be all right. Afterward, I was lying in a daze on a bed in the recovery room when the nurse—a large black woman with the face of an angel—came over to see how I was doing.

Once she determined that my vitals looked okay, she leaned in to whisper quietly, "Honey, forgive me for prying, but you don't look like you have a lot of money, and I thought I'd let you know that they charge in ten-minute increments just for lying there."

I don't know how she figured out that I didn't have medical insurance, but her words were a much-needed blessing at that moment. As I looked into her kind face, I felt comforted and loved. She seemed to understand my grief in a way that I hadn't even begun to allow myself to experience. As she lightly touched my hand, a wave of compassion and warmth flowed from her fingertips into my body, and tears rolled down my cheeks . . . I was so grateful for the encounter. I thanked her, and even though I was still very weak, I made my way out of the hospital.

It took more than a month of staying in bed for my body to heal from the miscarriage and the massive loss of blood. We buried the tiny "fetus" in a big pot in our living room that held a ficus tree, and I slowly started to recover emotionally. During this period, I had a lot of time for contemplation—day after day I reclined on the couch and gazed at that ficus tree, which somehow seemed greener and more beautiful with each passing day. I was sure that the spirit of the baby was nourishing the plant.

Every day I grew more thankful for the experiences I'd had at the hospital. It was there that I was reminded of an important lesson in my life. I'd been shown that the Creator dwelled every-where—in the tiny fetus now slumbering at the base of our ficus tree, in the halls of hospitals, in the medication I'd been given, and in the hearts of nurses and doctors. This reminder that God dwells everywhere, even in the least likely places, has made an enormous difference in my life, and I'm now convinced that I can connect with the Source no matter where I am.

GOD EVEN DWELLS IN MEDICATION!

It may be easier to experience the sacred and holy in beautiful places—such as in nature, during a sunset or sunrise, or in a temple or sanctuary—than in ordinary life. Nevertheless, we still need to remember that the creative force is actually everywhere. This is always true, no matter who you are . . . no matter where you are . . . no matter what's happening in your life. Even in those places where you're certain that spiritual energy couldn't possibly live, *it does!* The Divine is only a thought away at all times. If you're open and willing to listen to its wisdom, the spirit world will reveal itself.

Since that time in the hospital, I've also come to believe that God can dwell in medications, too. For most of my adult life I wouldn't even take aspirin because it seemed unnatural—instead, I believed in wheatgrass juice, tofu, and organic living. I adamantly shunned medications of any kind. While I'm still an advocate of natural living, in the last few years I've come to understand that Spirit can exist in human-made things as well. I now appreciate ibuprofen, for instance, which is a miracle drug for me. My spine was damaged when I was shot—now whenever my back gives me problems, ibuprofen actually eases the pain and stops it from getting worse. What might have kept me in bed for a week hardly fazes me now.

I've also discovered other medications. Over the years, I've traveled many times to more than 20 countries to teach, and I've experienced severe jet lag. I tried everything to combat it, and homeopathy, melatonin therapy, circadian-rhythm tapes, aromatherapy, dowsing, energized water, and magnets all failed me. Once I even traveled with large copper plates taped to the top and bottom of my spine. Each plate was connected to copper wires, which I held in my hands during the entire flight. I felt absurd. (I can only imagine how I'd explain this to someone enforcing the heightened airport security we have today.) Even though I know that many others have had wonderful results with these remedies, none of them worked for me.

On a recent flight to Thailand, I decided to do something I would never even have considered while in my former mode of thinking. I took a sleeping pill. It was the first time ever, and I felt terribly guilty—as if I were betraying my allegiance to alternative medicine—but I slept through almost the entire 14-hour flight. When I finally landed in Chiang Mai, I hardly had any jet lag at all. Yet on the return flight, I acquiesced to my belief that I should avoid human-made drugs and decided not to take a pill. I ended up suffering with an extreme case of jet lag that lasted two weeks.

I certainly don't believe that taking sleeping pills, or any other drug for that matter, should become a way of life—holistic medicine can always be considered as an alternative and viable solution. However, I now know that medication, when used sparingly and responsibly, can be just as much a gift from God as clouds, sunsets, and rainbows.

STEPS TO EMPOWERMENT

Is there a place that you abhor visiting, or certain individuals whom you despise having to see because you associate them with negative experiences you've had in your life? Take a few moments to list anything that you have a poor attitude toward and consider why you have those feelings. Next, try to imagine yourself walking through that place or talking to one of those people, and be aware of your responses.

Slowly introduce the idea that the Divine Source is there with you by imagining that the spiritual realm surrounds the space you're standing in or the person you're talking to, and notice how this impacts the way that you feel. You might even want to affirm: *I stand in my light, and I see Your magnificence.* Later, remind yourself of this exercise when you venture into that place you've always dreaded or come into contact with someone you usually try to avoid. You might even say to yourself *God* (or the Creator/Goddess/Great Mystery/Cosmic Consciousness/Divine Source/whatever word you choose) *is here, too.*

Remember that the world around you, including the people you meet and the experiences you have, always contain elements of the spiritual realm. The more you remind yourself that the Creator and the spirit world are in and around you as a part of everything, the more this truth will reveal itself to you.

Your Thoughts
Affect Your
Abundance

I was hungry—not starving like someone on the streets of New Delhi, but hungry nonetheless. There wasn't any food in the cupboard, and I didn't have any way to buy some. Even though I was newly married, I was often alone for many days at a time without money—and sometimes without much to eat.

My husband, David, and I had met in Hawaii; however, soon after we married, he insisted that we relocate to Northern California because he felt cooped up on the islands. David wanted to live in a place with more open space than could be found in Hawaii, so we moved into a tiny bungalow on an isolated cliff overlooking the cold and foggy Pacific Ocean.

It was wonderful at first . . . but as our meager savings ran out, it got tough. We were broke, and I often spent days alone in the house while David tried to get work in San Francisco (which was hours away). He'd often be gone for five or six days at a stretch, come home for a day or two on the weekends, and then head back to the city the following Monday. Although he'd bring groceries and supplies each time he returned, it was still hard to be away from him and live on so little for days with no car and no money to replenish our supplies.

This particular week, I hadn't been as careful with my food allotment as I could have been, and I ran out. I was hungry and could do nothing but wait for David to return that weekend. I hated the waiting—I was tired of being alone and cold in our damp, moldy cottage . . . and I was especially tired of not having enough to eat. I passed the time thinking about how happy I'd been in

Hawaii, where I had a great job and wonderful friends and the weather was warm and sunny. It was a far cry from the constant soggy chill that crept off the ocean into our sparsely furnished little cabin and slowly seeped into my bones.

I decided to go for a walk to pass the time. Eventually I plopped myself down on the cliff in disgust and looked out at the ocean. Tall grass was blowing in my face, and I was so miserable. I didn't know what to do. *God, I need help!* I prayed. *Right now I don't even know if You exist . . . but please, if You're real, help me now.* (When things were going well, I was sure of God's existence—it was only in the dark times that I doubted everything, including the existence of the Creator.)

After I finished my prayer, I just continued to sit there. I don't know what I expected—maybe I was hoping for pennies to fall from heaven or for an angel to appear . . . I don't know. I just needed something—anything—to happen, but nothing did. At that time in my young life, I didn't understand the power of faith or how we often need to be patient for prayers to be answered.

I was about to give up and head back to the house when a small breeze picked up. I was pulling my sweater around my shoulders to guard against the chill when something on the ground, a few steps away, caught my eye. The wind was tossing around a rolled-up piece of paper and blowing it in my direction. When it was just within my reach, the wind suddenly stopped, and the paper rested in the grass beside me. I reached out, picked it up, and unrolled . . . a dollar bill! Even though it was only a buck, to me it was a miracle. I could get something to eat!

A flurry of questions jangled through my head: *Where did it come from? How did it get there? Why did it stop just in front of me? Is this a gift from God?* I bounded to the road to hitch a ride to the nearest country store, which was about 20 minutes away. I was excited about the prospect of buying myself a loaf of bread and a small carton of milk.

As I waited for a ride, I kept thinking about the miracle of that dollar. It certainly solved my problem of being hungry and broke, but I started to wonder if maybe there was a deeper message in it. I remembered that old proverb "Give a man a fish and you feed him for a day. Teach a man to fish and you feed him for a lifetime." Maybe the dollar bill had been blown in my direction to be my "fishing pole" rather than my "fish."

Before I spent it, I stared at the dollar clinched between my fingers. I realized that although it was just a green piece of paper—that in and of itself could do little but start a fire—it was the meaning placed on it that made it valuable. *Money is energy!* The thought struck me like a thunderbolt. *And if it's energy, I can influence it with my thoughts and beliefs!*

Realizations about money poured out of me: *The difference between $1 and $100 is a couple of zeros, and what are zeros but empty space? I can create more money out of the empty space with my thoughts!* Once I realized that money was only energy, I also understood that there was nothing to worry about anymore. Although there were many times in those early years of our marriage when David and I had very little cash, I consider that day as the turning point in our journey toward abundance. We now live a prosperous life, which I believe all started to be put into motion by the tumbling "runaway dollar"—and the realizations that tumbled to me along with it.

THINK AND GROW RICH

How we relate to money has a huge impact on how we experience prosperity. In other words, if we feel and act abundant—even if we're really not—then we'll prosper in all areas of our life.

Our abundance level emerges from our beliefs about what we deserve. For example, research has been done on lottery winners who were given a lump sum of money, and the results aren't so surprising: Those who were middle-class before they won were still middle-class three years later, those who were poor before they won were poor again within three years, and those who were rich to begin with stayed rich. *The amount of money that they started with was generally what they had three years later!*

This research points to the notion that we human beings have a zone where we feel comfortable, and most of us don't tend to venture beyond it. It can be compared to an internal thermometer—if we have less than we feel we deserve, it's as if a heater comes on to warm things up to where we feel comfortable. However, if we find ourselves in a situation where we have more than we subconsciously feel that we deserve, then the air-conditioning engages to cool things back down. We may even sabotage ourselves until we return to that comfort zone.

STEPS TO EMPOWERMENT

It's not what you consciously feel you deserve that controls your prosperity—it's what you believe *sub*consciously that controls it. Once you understand your comfort level, you can work toward raising it, and consequently elevate your *abundance* level.

To discover the range where you feel comfortable, look at what you have . . . this is a tried-and-true way to tell. Also, visualize yourself at different levels of abundance: Notice where it starts to feel uncomfortable, both when you feel that you're *lacking* it and also when you feel that you have more than you need. For example, perhaps your image of someone with a lot of money is associated with having a housekeeper—but when you visualize *yourself* with a housekeeper, it feels uncomfortable. This might indicate that your comfort level is below this point. To push through to the next one, continue to see yourself at a particular income level and keep visualizing elements of living at this level until it feels absolutely comfortable and even joyous. The more you do this type of visualization, the easier it is to manifest more abundance in every area of your life!

Cherish Yourself

A few years ago, I was diagnosed with breast cancer. I immediately went into shock and complete denial. It scared me—I mean *really* scared me—and I didn't want anyone else to know. When I *could* finally talk about it, I realized that the disease was a sign that I needed to take stock of my life. It may sound like a cliché, but there's nothing like facing death to make you aware of what's important in life.

The possibility that I might soon be dead gave me an incredibly valuable tool to make choices in my life. I was no longer concerned with what was happening with my career or material possessions, nor did I fear failure or humiliation or worry about doing what others expected of me—all of these concerns paled in comparison to what I was dealing with in the face of death. I began to discern what was really meaningful to me and started following the dictates of my heart. I no longer had a valid reason *not* to follow my bliss.

When I took a serious look at how I felt about my life, I was surprised to discover that I was actually willing to die—if that was my fate, I would accept it. My daughter, Meadow, was out of college and had entered the working world, and although I knew she'd be heartbroken if I died, I was confident that she'd eventually be all right. I knew my husband, David, would also be very sad, but I felt that he'd ultimately get beyond it, too.

The next question I asked myself was much harder, *Am I ready to really live?* As I did so, I began to understand that the arrival of cancer was only a symptom of a much deeper problem. I realized that in order to *really* live, I needed to make some big changes in my life. I knew that I was going to have to change some old patterns.

For example, I'd always been a people pleaser. I often made decisions based on what others wanted from me, rather than listening to my own needs. Despite the immense amount of personal growth I'd worked on for decades, this negative pattern still greatly affected my life. So I asked myself if I was ready to make the changes necessary to start living that life. *Am I willing to stop putting other people's needs ahead of mine? Am I ready to let go of the need to please everyone? Can I stop taking care of everyone else and start taking care of myself?* These weren't easy questions to answer.

Meanwhile, the doctors wanted me to come back in for more tests and start receiving treatment, but I wanted to wait and ponder my options. I felt that I still needed time to do some deep soul-searching to see if there were any other submerged issues that might be contributing to the cancer.

Then one day it hit me—I needed to stop waiting! I'd been waiting my whole existence for my real life to begin. I'd been looking forward to happiness, convincing myself that I couldn't experience it because I didn't have the time, the money, or the energy, or because my schedule was too rigid to allow for it. I kept thinking that someday in the future, when conditions were perfect, the delaying would be over and I'd be happy.

In high school, I thought that when I moved out and was far away from the violence and upheaval at home, I'd finally be happy and my life would begin. However, when I moved out, nothing changed. Then I thought that when I went to college I'd be happy, but that didn't happen either. After graduation, I told myself that once I had a job in the real world, then my life would commence— but it didn't. So I began to tell myself that my life would definitely start as soon as I got married. And guess what? That didn't do it either.

There was always some future goal or condition—like owning my own home, having a baby, writing a book, or traveling to other countries—that had to be fulfilled before my "real life" would begin. I thought that when I was done with my to-do list in life, I could relax and do what *I* wanted . . . I'd finally be happy. But I never got it all done, and consequently, I never attained my heart's desire. Instead, I went through life unable to relax and to truly enjoy where I was.

But now, confronted with cancer, I realized that happiness and joy was a path, not a destination, and they were to be found in how I lived each moment of my life. I realized that I didn't need to wait for everything to be perfect—I only needed to know that I was on the right path, regardless of what was happening around me. In fact, I'd *always* been on the right path, even when I didn't know it.

I saw that there's no way to joy . . . joy *is* the way. It's always available to us, no matter what's happening in our lives. When we stop postponing joy—until we lose ten pounds, become sober, earn a degree, get married, have kids, undergo plastic surgery, retire, get divorced, or win the lottery—we become privy to the secret that the way to happiness is to experience it now!

When cancer threatened my life, I saw that I might not have the luxury of waiting until the future unfolded to find my contentment. Since I knew that I had to find it in every present moment, I began to embrace life like I never had before. I cherished all of it—even the disappointment and sadness—because *everything* was worth celebrating. I began to love my life with every cell in my body.

A month after I'd had my first series of tests, I went back to the doctors . . . and to their complete surprise, they couldn't find *any* cancer. They speculated that they may have misdiagnosed me the first time, even though they'd previously had no doubts that I had the disease.

Either way—whether I'd had cancer or not—I was immensely grateful for the entire experience. In the strangest way, facing my own mortality was exactly what I needed to start living. It forced me to look at my life honestly and gave me the ability to experience joy *now,* not somewhere down the road. I now plunge into everything with passion. I laugh! I dance! I sing! And I refuse to take myself or anything that happens to me too seriously. I now see that seriousness is a sickness of the soul and that laughter brings energy back into the being.

SAVOR EVERY MOMENT

When you hurry through your day, you miss the joy that's always available to you, which is like throwing away a precious gift without ever opening it. Slow down . . . life isn't a race. Get up and take the time to dance—wildly, sensuously, and freely—before the song is over. Having inner peace doesn't mean that there's only serenity, harmony, and stillness around you or that there are never any difficulties, ups and downs, or tragedies. It does mean, however, that no matter what's going on around you, you know that there's a calm stillness in your heart that's radiant and forever. Having inner peace means that you enjoy the moment, and that above all else, you take time to cherish yourself—no matter what's happening.

Unfortunately, society teaches women from early childhood to postpone joy and sacrifice their needs for others'. Yet by trying to always be friends with everyone and putting other people first, we often sacrifice the well-being of our most important friend, the one who's always on our side—ourselves. Without that inner companionship, life isn't very fulfilling.

It takes immense courage to be our own best friends, but it's part of finding inner peace and living our lives to the fullest. In our culture, we're taught that it's okay to say things like "I love chocolate," "I love rainbows," or "I love hiking," but if you say "I love myself," there's often an uncomfortable silence. We're taught that loving ourselves is selfish and egotistical. I'm reminded of the time I told a journalist how I overcame cancer by loving myself. Upon hearing this, she became visibly uncomfortable, cut the interview short, and never published the article. I knew that I'd overstepped society's unspoken rule: One should never admit that they love themselves.

It takes courage to like and eventually *love* the person you are, and our culture doesn't always make it easy. But loving yourself is not only possible, it also has enormous implications with respect to the quality of your life. Give yourself a best friend for life—you—and cherish that friendship. Being your own best friend means that you always get to hang out with someone who thinks that you're great and can appreciate you just as you are right now.

STEPS TO EMPOWERMENT

As you grow older, your list of things to do "someday" may get longer than the number of days you have left. So start experiencing joy *today* by doing the things that make you happy. Take that account of what you want to accomplish one day and replace it with a list of ways that you're seizing the moment and enjoying life right now.

Start by asking yourself the following: *If I had only one month to live, what would I do differently? Whom would I call or spend time with? What would I say to them? What would I want to experience or share with someone?* Now ask yourself, *Why am I waiting?*

If, during your last month on Earth, you had to honestly evaluate yourself, take a moment to think about this:

- What do you like about yourself?

- What do you *love* about yourself?

- If another person had the exact same qualities that you possess, would you want to hang out with him or her?

- If you're not your own best friend, what do you need to do to nurture and to cherish this friendship?

It's time to try to become your own best friend! Approach the birth of a friendship with yourself as if you were cultivating a treasured relationship with another person. Would you take that buddy out for lunch, shopping, a massage, or a walk outside? Figure out what you'd do for your best pal—and then do it!

None of us can know when we'll be looking at our last rainbow or sunrise, or when it will be our last chance to see loved ones or tell them how much we care. So it's essential to take in every moment of life as though it were your last opportunity to have that experience. It's time to *carpe diem*—seize the day . . . no, seize the moment!—and live each day as if it were your last.

CHAPTER FIVE

Discovering What's Truly Important in Life

STRIVE FOR
EXCELLENCE . . .
NOT PERFECTION

I woke up early to the baleful moan of foghorns filtering through the early-morning mists of the San Francisco Bay. As I snuggled deeper into my down comforter, I hugged my knees to my chest and curled my toes. I loved listening to the long, lonely sounds of the foghorns while I was safe and warm in bed. Just as I was about to drop back into a delicious sleep, I remembered that David and I were having a dinner party that night, so I'd have to start getting ready for it. Reluctantly, I threw off the covers and ran across the chilly floor to the warmth of the bathroom.

We'd invited six people for dinner—three couples who also lived in the Bay Area—timing their arrival so that they could gather on the balcony and have a stellar view of the sunset while they sipped their wine. Our home in the Marina District of San Francisco might have been small, but it had a great balcony that overlooked the Golden Gate Bridge, the bay, and out to the Pacific Ocean beyond. This would surely be a great beginning for a perfect gathering.

I began to prepare for the soiree. I scrubbed the bathroom, cleaned the windows, vacuumed the rugs, swept the wood floors, dusted the shelves and tabletops, and raced around making sure that everything was sparkling clean. Then I headed out to run errands and pick up the necessities for the party: roses from a flower shop, bread from a French bakery, seafood from the fish market, wine from a local vendor, and vegetables from the grocery store.

After returning home, I bolted up and down the two flights of stairs to our flat. It took several trips to get all the groceries out of my car and upstairs. Once inside the apartment, I became a whirlwind—chopping, mincing, and cooking the food; and then trimming, arranging, and rearranging the flowers in vases. I put blossoms in every room and spent several minutes trying to decide exactly how to position each arrangement. I also wanted to make sure that the table was perfectly set, so I ironed the napkins into fancy designs, trimmed the wicks on the candles, laid out the dishes, and adjusted the silverware until everything seemed right.

I was so focused on the task of perfecting every little thing that I grumbled at David several times because I thought that he wasn't helping enough. We were newly married and had recently moved to San Francisco from our little bungalow in Northern California, and he didn't quite know what to make of me when I got into such a flurry. He was just trying to keep a safe distance from my frenetic activities and would say things like, "They're coming here to see *you,* not your house. What's the big deal?" I'd roll my eyes and keep working.

After all the preparations were done and the meal was ready, I started working on the details of getting myself ready. After I took a shower, I tried on five different outfits—I changed my mind so many times because nothing seemed quite right—until I felt that I had the appropriate outfit for the evening. Next I styled my hair, applied makeup, and chose jewelry. Once I was ready, I flew back into the living room, tested the stereo, selected the music, and decided on the order that I'd play the songs throughout the evening.

Just before everyone was scheduled to arrive, I took a moment to breathe and flopped down on the couch. I was exhausted, frustrated, and even a bit resentful. It sounds crazy, but I was a little irritated at everyone for how hard I'd worked to get everything ready for them. But then I was off and running again—as our guests arrived, I poured their wine and escorted them outside to enjoy the sunset. The fog had cleared and the setting sun was glorious. While they relaxed, I spent my time in the kitchen putting the finishing touches on the meal.

During dinner everyone was seated comfortably around the table, while I raced to and from the kitchen and brought out the courses. Back and forth . . . from the appetizers to the salads . . .

from the main course to the dessert and coffee. It was the "perfect" dinner party, but I barely had time to congratulate myself after everyone left before I noticed the huge stack of dishes looming in the kitchen. I felt depleted and depressed about the work I still had ahead of me. Sure, I'd hosted an amazing evening, but afterward I felt empty and unsatisfied. And it wasn't the first time. It seemed that I always wanted to do everything perfectly, yet I rarely experienced a sense of accomplishment for all the time and effort I put into it.

EXCELLENCE IS HERE AND NOW

When I asked myself why I always ended up feeling so lousy after every dinner party or event, I realized that it was because I was a perfectionist. Since perfection is a standard that can almost never be achieved, to strive for it is actually a setup for failure. I wanted to give my best to the world, but trying to be flawless was exhausting and even debilitating, so I have since decided to strive for *excellence* instead of perfection. This means that although I continue to raise my standards, I also enjoy myself along the way.

Right now, I'm a recovering perfectionist—sometimes I relapse, but I'm working on it. It's been a long and difficult journey as I go from *believing* that I have to do everything a certain way to *understanding* that it's a greater virtue to strive for excellence instead of perfection (excellence is *not* a synonym for perfection).

While trying to host a "perfect" dinner party leaves me exhausted, resentful, and unfulfilled, an "excellent" dinner party leaves me feeling nourished, appreciated, and loved. I walk away with the sense that I've spent quality time with friends and family, and I'm able to enjoy the preparation process *and* be relaxed and have fun during the meal.

I've discovered that I can create a memorable gathering, as well as spend quality time with cherished friends and family, by allowing them to share in the process with me. I allow them to bring things and even help with the last-minute details; in other words, I don't try to do it all myself anymore. I've also realized that people are coming to see me and not necessarily my home, so it's okay if the house isn't totally immaculate. I often make one great entrée and buy the rest premade, which leaves me more time with my guests and allows me to avoid being in the kitchen the entire evening. Finally, I let them help with the cleanup. Some people might find these things to be common elements of a dinner party, but it was a major realization for me that I could throw a wonderful gathering, event, or seminar without trying to be perfect . . . and I could have fun doing it!

This philosophy of choosing excellence over perfection can be applied to many other aspects of life. Striving for flawlessness demands all of your focus and takes your energy away from the enjoyment of the moment. You'll find that you attend to the details with so much effort that your mind is unable to relax or to enjoy the very details that you care so much about. Striving for excellence, on the other hand, is more about the intention than a preconceived result, and it also puts you in a healthier state of mind. I now *intend* to give the world my best, and at the same time, I *allow* myself to fully experience the joy in each moment. Helen Keller said, "When we do the best that we can, we never know what miracle is wrought in our life, or in the life of another"—to me, this is the spirit of excellence.

I believe that you always have a choice to enter into the energy of excellence. It begins with aligning your thoughts and words—the language you use with yourself and with others—to declarations that are empowering. For example, imagine that someone gives you a compliment about the way you look, your home, or a painting that you've done. Instead of responding with statements that deflect or minimize your abilities, such as, "Oh, you didn't see how I looked before I put my makeup on," "It doesn't usually look this good," or "I think these colors are too muddy"—all very perfection-conscious statements—replying with a simple "Thank you" comes from a place of excellence. It shows that you've tried to do your best and that you graciously accept the compliment for your efforts.

Additionally, excellence is not something in the future—it starts here and now. It's not about surpassing others or trying to be perfect; rather, it's about embracing all that's within and around you with gusto and joy, even when things don't go your way. It's about accepting that what you have now is worth celebrating, rather than lamenting because it's not more. It's seeing the best in yourself, in your life, and in others . . . and taking the time to cherish and enjoy it.

STEPS TO EMPOWERMENT

Life is unpredictable, and it can sometimes be messy. Things come up unexpectedly—we run out of time, we have bad-hair days, and sometimes the casserole gets overcooked. That's just the way it is. The key is not to get too caught up in little things. Rather than striving for some grand idea of perfection, just try to do the best you can with what you have at the time. You'll be surprised when it turns out to be pretty spectacular!

If you're like me and tend to imagine how things could be flawless—and you get unsettled when they're not—the challenge is to let go of those unattainable ideals. Just accept and embrace what your life has to offer, especially when it's messy. If there's an area of your life that's definitely not perfect, just say to yourself (and the world), "This is the way it is. Ta-da!"

Imagine that you have a bag of fresh lemons sitting on your counter and company coming over that night for a dinner party. Maybe you'd planned to make the most exquisite lemon tart ever created, but you ran out of time. Is all hope lost for the success of your party? Of course not! You can make homemade lemonade with a sprig of mint to serve to your guests, or you can just clean the fruit and place it on the coffee table in a decorative bowl. The key is to stop beating yourself up if the situation doesn't work out according to some grand plan. Accept it and look for the good. This is the first step to excellence. The next step is to see what you can do to improve the situation.

Always maintain the spirit of joy rather than the specter of judgment and discouragement in life. That way, when life gives you lemons . . . you'll know what to do. Make lemonade, of course!

God Is in the Details

It had been an unbelievably long day—one of those that had begun so early that it felt as if I'd woken up the day before, and even after the sun went down, it still had no foreseeable end. I was teaching a seminar to several hundred people in Canberra, Australia. We'd been in the conference room for so many hours that we needed cardigans and shawls to withstand the cold blasts coming out of the air-conditioning vents. It was a warm and sunny day outside, but you wouldn't have known it by looking around the room.

Each time I let the group take a break and stretch, get a snack, or run to the restroom, many stayed to speak to me one-on-one about the topics I'd covered. So I spent every break fielding questions from this particularly inquisitive group, and while the students had some time to catch their breath in between segments, I didn't. I was happy to answer additional questions, but it demanded that I engage with the seminar participants nonstop. By late afternoon, I hadn't had any sort of respite myself.

After the final break, the group took their seats and stared up at me expectantly. They were eagerly waiting for me to begin, but I realized that I really needed to use the restroom and it just couldn't wait. In fact, it was bordering on an emergency. After quickly weighing my options—while looking out at the people in the audience with their pens poised—I decided that it was better for me to ask them to wait for a few minutes than to try to finish the presentation uncomfortably.

"Thank you so much for coming back on time. We'll start in just a couple of minutes, but first there's something I've got to take care of. Please excuse me for a moment—I'll be right back," I explained to group. There was a bathroom just offstage, so I tried to be as quick as possible.

When I was done, I felt much better. I readjusted my clothing, stepped back onstage . . . and was met with uproarious applause as I walked toward the podium. It was as if I'd just won an Academy Award, and I smiled broadly. *Wow! They must really be enjoying the seminar,* I thought with pleasure and pride. Then, en masse, everyone rose to their feet and gave me a heartfelt, standing ovation. The sound was deafening!

I nodded my head and accepted the applause, trying to look as humble as possible, while I was secretly overjoyed. "Thank you! Thank you," I said into my microphone. "You're so kind."

I then heard muffled laughter from several areas of the room. That's when someone approached the stage and whispered in my ear, "You forgot to turn off your wireless microphone when you went to the bathroom. *We heard everything!"*

Suddenly a horrific visual image filled my mind as I recounted my last few moments in the bathroom. *Oh my God!* I realized. *They heard all of that!* I can't imagine how many shades of red I must have turned as I stood there, but there was little else to do but join everyone in laughter and then carry on with my talk.

EVEN THE LITTLE THINGS ARE TOUCHED BY GOD

Over the years, I've learned the importance of details. The simple act of turning off my microphone before going to the bathroom, for instance, would have saved me from an embarrassing moment. Sometimes it's the small things, such as remembering to change the oil in our cars, reseal a paint can, or recharge a cell phone that can have the biggest consequences or the most far-reaching effects on our lives.

In the past, I viewed details as restraints that bogged me down and held me back from being free and from doing what I really wanted to do. Over time, however, I've come to realize that attending to them actually gives me more freedom, more time, and less restriction overall in my life. For example, when I remember to take coins for the parking meter when I run errands, I don't have to make an additional trip to the bank to get change and then hurry back to the car to fill the meter. The more details I can take care of, the simpler my life actually feels.

A spiritual revelation occurred for me when I began to conduct ceremonies for space clearings, weddings, births, deaths, and rites of passage. I started to fully grasp the importance of even the littlest things. It's not only important to remember the large items, such as a marriage license for a wedding ceremony or the proper tools for a space clearing, it's also essential to attend to the seemingly insignificant parts as well. God is even in these small details, and paying attention to them can actually bring us closer to the Creator. To me, a successful ceremony isn't one that just looks or sounds good, it's one in which the Divine is present. When every part of a ritual is attended to deliberately, from the freshness of the flowers to a well-trimmed wick on a candle, the experience is more whole—therefore, it's easier for Spirit to infuse every aspect of the ceremony. You can usually feel when it's close: Since its presence is very tangible and real, you can feel energy in the air, which resonates in your heart.

No matter what your big goal is, paying attention to the details while releasing the need to be perfect will expand and improve your life. For example, if you want to be healthier in general, focus on all the minute aspects of your well-being: Take your vitamins every day, be conscious of what you eat and drink, floss daily, and treat your body with respect and reverence.

Similarly, if you want to have a lush and abundant garden, start by planting strong, healthy, and high-quality seeds or plants in good soil. Water them as much as is necessary and feed them the best nutrients. Pull the weeds, and protect your harvest from bugs, slugs, and birds. Paying attention to the small details contributes to the overall sustenance of the space.

The message is this: When you take care of the little things and recognize them as being touched by God, everything will resonate with a magical energy, and you'll enjoy your experiences to the fullest.

Steps to Empowerment

What area of your life do you want to enhance? Is it health, abundance, relationships, creativity, adventure, or inner peace? Write down your overall goals on a piece of paper or in a journal, and then list seven different details for each one that you could attend to in order to make that dream a reality.

After you've made your list, take action by rolling up your sleeves and experiencing the nitty-gritty. Pay attention to even the tiniest details that relate to your overall goal, thinking small rather than big. The magic behind this approach is that by taking care of the tiny steps, you're actually starting to take very big leaps toward realizing your goal.

Carry around your lists of the little things you'd like to complete, and also schedule when you'll do each one. Think through how you'll do them—even draw pictures or maps if that would help you gain clarity about the process. Then get to work on crossing them off your list, and watch with joy as you see your overall goal becoming a reality as well.

Begin It Now

When I was in my 20s, I couldn't imagine anything in the world more fulfilling than being an author. Then one day when I was 34, I received a call from a small publishing company asking me to write a book. They'd heard about my seminars and thought that my popularity as a public speaker would attract people to my books as well. It was a dream come true . . . but instead of being thrilled and getting right to work, I panicked. Every time I thought about it, my heart fluttered and my mouth went dry. I couldn't understand why I was so upset until I realized that it's much easier to yearn for a seemingly impossible dream than to confront the reality of actually writing a book.

For days I stared at my computer screen. Whenever I'd finally write something, I'd read it over, become dismayed at how terrible it was, and then delete it. Realizing that I'd never get the book written that way, I decided to go to a therapist to get help with my writer's block. "I stupidly said yes when I was asked to write a book," I confessed. "The truth is I'm a lousy writer. I don't have enough education to do it. They want me to give them a manuscript about dreams, but I'm not really an expert. I need more training . . . I don't think that I know enough to write a book."

I sank deeper and deeper into depression with each concern that I shared with her. When I was done, she looked at me thoughtfully and said, "Denise, I don't think you're going to like my advice, but here it is: Be willing to do it badly—just get it done."

"What?" I responded in shock. "You have a master's degree from Harvard and you're telling me to do it badly?"

"Yes, that's what I said. Be willing to do a lousy job. Just do it," she affirmed with an unyielding look in her eye.

I stumbled out of the therapist's office shaking my head in disbelief. I thought that we'd uncover my childhood blockages or discuss my self-esteem issues—I never expected such simplistic advice. Yet the next morning as I sat at my computer, I was determined to try out her advice to write a lousy book. And amazingly, the words just poured out of me.

Less than one month later, I'd finished my first manuscript, which I titled *Pocketful of Dreams* (in the United States it's called *The Hidden Power of Dreams*). And you know, it's not that bad of a book. In fact, it's still in print today, 20 years later. What's more, I continue to receive letters and e-mails from people who say that it's their "dream bible."

Be Willing to Do It Badly—Just Get It Done

I now realize what wonderful advice this wise therapist gave me. I'd been so worried that I wouldn't write perfectly that I couldn't even start, and she gave me permission to get it done by telling me that it was all right to do it badly.

If we keep waiting until we take that perfect first step, we'll find ourselves forever on one leg. It's like toddlers learning to walk—in the beginning, they stumble and fall over and over until they finally get the hang of it. We'd never think of telling these small children, "Hey, you didn't do it perfectly, so just give it up. Or better yet, don't even try." And just as we'd never speak this way to kids, we shouldn't do it to ourselves either. We don't have to be perfect; we just have to start. We can always make corrections and improve the process after we've gained momentum.

Many years ago, a friend of mine started her own newspaper. The first issue was terrible—the grammar was poor, the layout was sloppy, and the photo quality was inconsistent. I was embarrassed for her, and mutual friends were horrified that she didn't wait until her publication was more professional before she shared it with the public.

My budding-journalist friend took me aside one day and said, "If I waited until my paper was perfect, I never would have gotten started at all. I knew that I just had to do it."

Every issue got better . . . and I'm happy to report that she eventually published a first-rate newspaper, interviewed famous personalities and heads of state, and even won a prestigious award for excellence. But none of this would have happened if she'd waited until it was perfect or she became an expert in publishing.

Once you take the first few steps, *then* you can make corrections. After all, you learn as you do the work. Even in something as precise as rocket science, it's interesting to note that after a rocket has launched, it can be off course 90 percent of the time. Luckily, rockets are programmed to constantly adjust their course while in flight, so they eventually reach their destination. It's the same with the work we do ourselves—we can make a correction in flight, but we need to get off the ground first.

Just as my friend got her newspaper established and *then* worked to make it better by adjusting and improving it as she went, if there's something that you've wanted to do, don't hesitate—just do it. Be willing to do it badly, and remember that you can make corrections as you go . . . but you must have something to correct first. Get to work on your dreams and take action, even if it looks like a first draft of what you imagined. When you do so, the universe will respond and will propel you in the direction of your goal.

STEPS TO EMPOWERMENT

What have you been putting off? Do you have a dream that's been sitting on the sidelines for a while? Do you imagine being a tough tennis competitor, but you never make it to the court because you're embarrassed by your lack of skill? Do you give up on cooking gourmet meals because you tend to burn everything you put in the oven?

It's time to try changing your approach. While it can be helpful to visualize yourself as an excellent chef, an elite athlete, or a best-selling author, it's important not to let this get in the way of your beginning. Be comfortable with the fact that you're not there yet, and remind yourself that there's only one way to get there—just start, and then get better as you go.

Get yourself off the sidelines and take a look at how you can make progress today. Take action—head to the court and assume that you'll send tennis balls flying in every direction, but if you keep hitting them, you *will* improve. Start cooking and keep trying ingredients; after all, your recipes can always be tweaked a little the next time to make them even better. Action builds momentum, and it will take you in the direction of your dreams. Start now . . . even if it isn't perfect or you do it badly . . . just do it now.

YOUR PEER GROUP
CAN DETERMINE
YOUR DESTINY

There are so many competing theories about how we become who we are. Some people think that our genetic makeup determines our identity, while others are certain that our childhood experiences shape us into the adults we become. I've also heard it said that our natural environment acts upon us in ways that create our sense of self. In addition to genetics, childhood and cultural programming, and the environment we live in, I believe that some of the strongest determinants of our own sense of identity are the definitions—both good and bad—that are assigned to us by our friends and peer groups.

Recently my daughter, Meadow, and I were on a long drive back home from San Francisco. It's a trip that I always enjoy, as the road winds its way through miles of verdant vineyards and oak-covered hills, with the Santa Lucia Mountains in the background. On this particular day, the reflection of the sun on the shiny grape leaves gave the fields a silvery sheen. It was a great backdrop for our intimate discussion.

Somewhere along the way, the grapes themselves found their way into the conversation when Meadow brought up the subject of wine. She mentioned that during a recent visit with some family friends who didn't drink much, she'd consumed a glass of wine at dinner and a beer at the picnic lunch the next day. Since no one else had been drinking, and she'd truly enjoyed both libations, she began to worry that these people thought she was a bit of a lush. She even began to think of herself as someone who might have imbibed excessively.

Then Meadow also pointed out another occasion when she'd had the opposite experience. She'd gone camping with some friends on an isolated beach nestled along the redwood coast, and since it was a cold day, they'd all sat around the driftwood campfire. While her friends were making crazy cocktails and throwing them back all afternoon, Meadow had only a beer or two as she stretched and relaxed on the sand. Later that evening, she had another one with the group while they continued to party late into the night. In their company, she'd felt as if she were barely drinking, and she wondered whether she was a prude.

It was interesting that in both situations, my daughter drank about the same amount—yet with our family friends, she saw herself as a "heavy drinker," while among her camping friends, she thought that she was a "prude." She and I then began to contemplate the extent to which each person's self-image is determined by the views of those around them.

I considered how much of my own identity was dependent upon my peer group. When I was younger, I surrounded myself with individuals who didn't cherish me—as a result, my already low self-esteem only declined more. It wasn't until I began to associate with others who valued me and who believed in my potential that I began to see myself in a better light. So now when I'm around people who see the best in me, I respond in kind. However, when I'm with those who are critical of me and judge my choices in life, I begin to doubt who I am and what I'm capable of doing. I'd like to think that *I* shape my own identity, but I know that my peer group dramatically influences how I regard myself.

YOU ARE DEFINED BY WHOM YOU SPEND TIME WITH

Your friends have a huge impact on your identity and can even influence your destiny, because your future is largely determined by how you see yourself. People who have a strong and confident identity are more likely to have an inspiring, bright future than those who constantly demean themselves. And guess what? Self-assured individuals are usually surrounded by others who can see their strengths. Similarly, with the help of a strong peer group, *you* can achieve far beyond your wildest expectations. But on the flip side, if your friends continually smash your hopes and dreams, you'll have a difficult time reaching your goals. It'll feel like trying to win a footrace while having a boulder tied around your waist.

One of the fastest ways to enhance your destiny is to stay around positive people who share your values and respect you. If you have a peer group that doesn't back you up or celebrate your successes, try to distance yourself from them. It's better to have no friends (or only one who believes in you) than a pack of people who don't support you. The faster you can disassociate yourself from any unhealthy acquaintances, the faster you'll manifest your heart's desire.

For example, for a number of years I had an employee who didn't think well of me. She grumbled if I asked her to do something, she chose her own hours and wouldn't let me know when she was coming in (or even if she was coming in at all), and she felt that it was her job to make the major decisions in my office. If I was mulling over concepts for a book, for instance, she'd tell me that my ideas were bad and that what *she* thought was much better. She made me doubt my own ability to come up with good subject matter for my work—I convinced myself that she was right about my abilities, and I told myself that I was grateful that she had such a knack for seeing all my flaws.

This woman continually talked about the manuscript that she was going to write and got angry whenever I received letters praising my books. I told myself that she was so organized and such a fast typist that I couldn't do without her—but what I failed to notice was the negative impact she was having on my self-esteem. I can now see how she was most likely compensating for her lack of confidence by constantly judging me; nevertheless, my feelings about my own strengths suffered, and doubt emerged as a result of her criticism. Looking back, I can't believe that I didn't fire her. I continued to work with her despite the negativity she brought into my life, and I felt worthless when I was around her . . . *yet I was the one who'd hired her!*

I should have chosen to distance myself from my employee, but it was only when my family and I moved out of state that she was no longer a negative force in my life. Without her around, my own feelings about myself were able to flourish—I witnessed my health improve significantly, my career expand greatly, and our financial prosperity increase dramatically. In addition, my relationship with David and Meadow strengthened deeply, and my general level of happiness grew exponentially. It was remarkable!

When I saw how different my life was without this woman's diminishing influence, I realized that I would never again allow someone to damage my life in that manner. I swore to myself that I *would not* associate with someone who didn't bring out the best in me. I now have friends and employees who are kind and supportive and believe in me. It makes a huge difference in every arena of my life.

If someone in *your* life doesn't believe in you, support you, and care for you . . . run, don't walk, to get out of the situation. And if you can't get that person out of your life, do whatever you can to diminish his or her impact on you. You're dramatically influenced by whomever you spend time with, so choose those individuals who see you in loving ways.

Additionally, pick a peer group that will challenge you to reach your potential and expand beyond whatever self-imposed barriers you may face. Let's say that you want to own your own business, for instance, but all your friends work for corporations and think that the idea of going out on your own is preposterous—well, they're not going to bring you any closer to your goal. Instead, look for a group of friends who also run their own businesses, and associate with them. They'll believe in you and help you. They might also know some of the pitfalls of self-employment, and may even be able to connect you to the right people as you work to establish yourself.

Another example would be that you want to become more prosperous, but all your friends have money issues or strong negative beliefs about people who are abundant. You may find it very difficult to get ahead financially because this peer group is always discouraging you. However, if your friends don't have blockages regarding their own wealth, and they don't negatively judge those who have more money than they do, *you'll* have a much easier time reaching your own financial goals.

STEPS TO EMPOWERMENT

Please take a moment to answer the following questions honestly and carefully:

- Do you feel supported and empowered by your friends, family, and peers?

- Who in your life really supports and empowers you?

- Are you happy with your identity? If not, think about your friends and ask yourself if they'd be upset with you if you changed it.

- Could you step into a new identity and still fit in with your peer group, or would it be difficult?

- Are in you in a stagnant but comfortable lull with your friends, or do they stimulate and challenge you to grow and stretch?

- If you're not happy with your peer group, what kind of person would you need to be to attract one that you'd like?

If it would be a challenge to step into your current peer group with a stronger, more confident identity, then you might consider a few modifications. If you've fallen into a dull, lackluster routine with your friends, it might be time to make some adjustments. Keep in mind that if you do decide to change or expand your peer group, you can do it in a loving, gentle way—it doesn't need to be hard or disruptive. This fine-tuning of your circle of friends and your environment will improve your own self-image—and ultimately enrich your life.

Your Outer Vestige
Can Influence
Your Future

In earlier times, Westerners would have called him a witch doctor. When I met him, I just called him remarkable. (In reality, he was a *sangoma,* the African equivalent of a Native American medicine man.) I was teaching in South Africa when I was asked if I'd like to spend time with a sangoma named Credo Mutwa, the spiritual head of all the Zulus in Africa. He was a sangoma of the highest level.

My journey to his village was long and arduous—and potentially dangerous—during the time when South Africa was in a state of limbo. It was just before the presidential elections in which Nelson Mandela was a candidate, and no one knew what was going to happen. There was talk of impending mass riots and outbreaks of violence, and there had already been numerous carjackings. In fact, it wasn't uncommon to hear about people who were pulled from vehicles during carjackings and shot so that there would be no witnesses.

My friend Amber, who was driving me to Credo's village, was armed. As two females driving alone through isolated parts of the country, we knew that were taking a chance—so Amber, a native of South Africa, made sure that we had a gun to protect ourselves. As we drove, she told me that if any men stepped in front of the car, I shouldn't be alarmed if she hit the gas and looked like she was going to hit them . . . because she was. It was a defensive tactic to avoid getting carjacked.

It was evening when we arrived at the *kraal* (village), and I took in my surroundings. In the evenings, the African bush is saturated with the sounds of droning insects; wild-animal calls; and the high-pitched, piercing cries of birds settling in for the night. Inside the mud and straw walls of his hut, Credo was clothed in animal skins, and a vast array of bones and talismans circled his neck. Sitting on the dirt floor around a fire that lit up the dried-clay walls of his abode, I listened to him late into the night as he spoke of ancient prophecies and recounted tribal stories.

Feeling like I'd stepped out of time, I went to sleep dreaming of vast spaces and a sky full of stars that stretched forever. The next day, during a special ceremony that Credo performed in my honor, I was told that my healing abilities were substantial and my gifts would be needed in the years ahead. I was given the African name *Nogukini*, which he said meant "the one who sees far beyond the stars." Even though I'd been working as a healer and had been leading seminars for many years, it was still humbling to hear this declaration by such a spiritual man.

The events that day consisted of lots of singing and dancing. At the height of the ceremony, Credo presented me with a Native American headdress that he'd been given 25 years earlier by a visiting chief from the United States. He said that he wanted me to have it because he felt certain it was time for it to be returned to the United States. Credo also feared for its safety in Africa—there had been a number of attempts on his life, and he was worried that if he were killed, it might be destroyed.

The moment my new friend placed the headdress on my head, an image of my Cherokee grandmother came into my mind and a wave of happiness rolled over me. Although female Native Americans traditionally didn't do so, she was known to wear a full headdress on occasion (although she usually wore only a single turkey feather in her hair). As I sat proudly with my spine straight and my head crowned with the red, white, and black feathers, I wondered if she was watching from the spirit lands. I was curious about what she thought of her granddaughter wearing a headdress, but I imagined that she felt proud.

It was a considerable undertaking to travel through Africa with a full Native American headdress. I didn't want to damage it in my suitcase, so when I stayed at a hotel, I put it upright on the desk or coffee table. Because of its presence in my room, I was treated deferentially by the native African staff in every hotel I stayed.

Evidently, the only person who would have carried something like that—even though it was a Native American item—would have been some kind of witch doctor. Several people asked me for healing potions or to tell them their fortune, and I received one desperate note under my door, presumably from a hotel maid, that read in broken English: "My boyfrind look at other womin. I need poshon [potion] to mak him stop. Pleas help."

When I returned to my room after being out for the day, there would often be a pile of offerings surrounding the headdress. I soon came to understand that this tribute was the native African way of honoring the shaman who wore it. It seemed that by my possessing something considered to be sacred, I was regarded as a sanctified being as well. I began to wonder if there was more power in external items than I had previously realized.

DRESS FOR SUCCESS

Sometimes in the privacy of my home, I took my headdress down off the shelf and carefully put it on, noting that it made me feel stronger, wiser, and more grounded. I don't think that there was anything magical about it—it just made me feel that way. Simply having the headdress in my possession set me up as a kind of sangoma. If I'd worn it in public in Africa, it might have inspired a kind of awe and respect from the residents there.

At that point, I began to pay attention to how the clothes I wore made me feel. Although it's my essence that distinguishes me, not what I wear, I discovered that my wardrobe does have a potent effect on how I feel . . . and how I feel often dictates the circumstances of my life. For example, if I wear outfits that make me feel strong and confident, people treat me accordingly. Yet when I wear old, sloppy clothes, not only do they make me feel a bit slovenly or even tired, but my life is also not as crisp and sparkling as it can be.

I've come to realize that what I wear can even help shape my future. If there's a quality—such as joy, vitality or success—that I desire to increase in the future, I've found that wearing apparel that enhances this feeling actually helps to bring that quality into my life.

Once I was asked to speak about feng shui to 300 architects and architecture students at a large university. I felt out of my league in this setting, but then I thought, *How would someone dress who was confident about speaking here? What can I wear that will make me feel comfortable in this environment?* I knew that people dress in a multitude of ways at a university, but what was important was that I dressed in a manner that felt great to *me*. I chose a black suit with a white scarf and medium heels, which felt stylish yet credible and professional. My self-esteem was high while I spoke, and I received rousing applause at the end of my talk. If I wore the normal, flowing, comfortable clothes I often don, I don't think I would have felt as confident.

Over time, I noticed that the feelings that various clothes gave me lasted long after I was no longer wearing them. In other words, I still maintained the feeling of confidence, courage, strength, femininity, poise, self-assurance, or grace given to me by what I'd chosen to wear—somehow the items had helped to imprint various qualities into me. The old maxim that "clothes make the man" may be hackneyed and trite, but my experience has made me feel that there actually is some truth to it.

Steps to Empowerment

To choose the best clothes to influence your destiny, first determine what you desire for yourself in your future. For example, if you yearn to have a life filled with adventure, dress like someone who's always ready to take risks and who does things on the spur of the moment. If your dream is to be prosperous, dress like someone who's abundant. And keep in mind that you can interpret these clothing styles however you want. (That is, wearing "something abundant" doesn't necessarily mean it has to be expensive.) Try it and see what happens.

Although your clothing is only one of many things that make you who you are, it's possible that what you wear can change the way you feel . . . and changing how you feel can transform the circumstances of your life.

CHAPTER SIX

Pathways
to Inner Peace

TUNING IN TO
INNER REALMS

Some of the days of my past are gone forever from my memory. They simply dissolved over time. Others linger in the recesses of my mind, a bit blurred and smudged at the edges. But then there are some moments that shimmer and sparkle in my recollection like the sun rising over an undulating sea. These memories are crisp and richly colored in detail. For example, even though I was only four years old, I remember one such brightly burnished day when my family bought our first television to our home in the central coast of California. We were one of the first families in our neighborhood to get one.

The events of the day that TV appeared in my living room are still as clear to me as the day they happened. On the early morning of this monumental date, sunshine poured through my bedroom window and awakened me before anyone else. Although the heat would later rise to 100 degrees, the morning temperature had been cooled by the night's ocean breezes and was perfect. For a while I lay and watched a spider overhead as she rolled up an insect in her web, but soon I became bored and jumped out of bed.

When I came out to the living room, I realized that no one else was up yet, and the house was still very quiet. But there, on the dining room table, was a strange glass-and-plastic box that hadn't been there when I went to bed the night before. I'd never seen anything like it—it had an opaque window with knobs on one side, and trailing out the back was a cord that was plugged into the wall. I sat next to it and tried to peer into the glass window, but I couldn't see anything. I ran my hand across the glass, which was smooth and cool to the touch.

Then I fingered one of the knobs, feeling the little ridges around its edge. Squeezing it between my fingers, I turned it sharply to the right. Instantly a loud noise belched from the box, and I jumped back. I heard people talking and looked around the room, but no one was there. All of a sudden, images began to appear in the window and come into focus. In amazement I watched as tiny people walked around and talked to each other inside of the box.

"Hey! Hi, everyone!" I shouted and waved my hands at the little people. Oddly, they didn't seem to hear me or to see me, so I shouted again, "Hi! It's me! Can't you hear me? I want to play with you!"

I knocked on the glass window, but they still ignored me. I thought that there must be a door into their house, so I walked around to the back of the box and tried to find a way to reach in and get the little guys to come out and play with me.

I was devastated when I later found out that there wasn't really anyone in the magic box. My parents laughed about it and told their friends how their daughter thought that there were little people in the television, which made me feel extremely embarrassed. I didn't want anyone to think I was dumb, so when my fifth birthday arrived, I declared to everyone that I was a big girl who knew that people didn't really live inside the TV. I laughed about how that was something silly that only babies believed. Secretly, however, I still felt that the television was magical and that tiny human beings lived inside of it. When no one was around, I continued to try to find a way to play with them.

I think that my first experience with TV instilled in me the belief that we can connect with other people and places by simply turning a dial. When I rotated that knob, I could instantly see people who were living thousands of miles away . . . and I could even see individuals who were no longer living! As a child, I was mystified by the idea of connecting with distant lands and individuals without ever leaving the comfort of my own living room.

I expanded upon this idea as a ten-year-old, when I stayed with my grandparents while my mother was in a mental hospital. During the two years I lived with my grandmother—who was an astrologer, numerologist, and mystic of sorts—I learned many things that fueled my understanding of realms beyond what we can see with our eyes. Grandma expanded my beliefs by telling me that I had psychic abilities, saying that all I had to do was "tune in" in order to access other realms and experience the magical elements of the world. It was interesting to hear her use the same words that the little people had on TV: "*Tune in* next week to find out what happens. . . ." She told me that simply by being still and tuning in, I could view the past and future and even speak to those who'd passed on. Grandma would also often share "messages" from beyond—her voice would lower and her eyes would glaze over as she transmitted them. I was in complete awe of her abilities.

My parents, who were both scientists and atheists, had encouraged me to question religion and spirituality, and they would have been horrified if they'd been aware of what Grandma was teaching me. Yet I had no problem accepting her words as truth. Although at times she struck me as a bit strange, I always felt as though she had much to teach me. And as an adult, I've found great joy in further developing the skills that she first saw and nurtured in me.

TURNING YOUR INNER DIALS

We each have dials—very much like those on a TV or radio—within ourselves that we can use to tune in to other realms and alternate dimensions. It's simply a matter of taking the time to be still and find our own internal frequency activators. Once found, these dials can be slowly and gently "turned" to tap in to numerous dimensions.

Just as you turn the dial on your radio to get classic rock, jazz, country, or news, you can also tune in to various inner frequencies. These spiritual channels are very distinct and specialized. Some can allow you to view ancient times or "talk" to those who have passed on; other windows in the ethereal spectrum can allow you to observe the future (these otherworldly conduits can also help you hear the messages from the trees, animals, and stones); and finally, there are mystical pathways that, when followed, can activate intuition and creativity.

A number of years ago, I spontaneously thought of a woman whom I hadn't seen in more than 15 years. We'd been friends but had lost track of one other, so I decided to use my inner-frequency activator to "dial" her station just to see if I could find her. During my meditation, I thought of her and then imagined that I was tuning my inner dial until there was only a clear image of her without any static.

I "saw" that she was unhappy and struggling in her life—sadness radiated all around her like a clinging gray cloud—so I sent light and love to her in my thoughts. After I completed my meditation, I decided to track her down. With a fair amount of research, I was able to locate her number and give her a call. She was thrilled to hear from me because her husband had died, and she'd been in a prolonged period of grieving. She told me that she'd kept wishing to talk to me . . . and was astonished when I called. We had a long conversation, and she said that she felt much better as a result.

I believe that I was able to make this connection with my friend in part because my grandmother had shown me how to use my abilities to do so, but also because of the way that first TV had shaped my early understanding of "seeing" people.

Steps to Empowerment

The first step to viewing other dimensions, places, and people is to believe that you can do it. And you can . . . anyone can. It can be difficult to "see" if you're experiencing tension or stress, so the second step for tuning your own inner dials is to become very relaxed. The best way to do so is to begin by watching your breath. Sit in a comfortable position and slowly breathe in and out, and observe yourself doing this for a while. You may also find the following ancient method helpful for calming and quieting your mind:

Once you're relaxed, place your awareness in the center of your forehead. Imagine that a violet ray of light is flowing in and out of a small opening there. You might want to imagine this stream of light being like an ocean wave that ebbs and flows, in and out. (This area of your forehead is called "the third-eye area," and many mystical traditions believe it to be the seat of the soul.) Match the flow of this light with the inhalation and exhalation motion of your breath. Each time you breathe in, inhale the violet light. With each exhalation, feel your body release all stress and tension.

Now focus on what you wish to see. For example, if you want to talk to a tree, imagine that it's in front of you. If it doesn't appear clear or seems vague, then visualize tuning an inner dial until the image or feeling becomes vivid and sharp in detail, and then imagine that you can hear what the tree has to say to you. If you want to talk to someone who's passed over, visualize this person standing in a beautiful place in nature such as the seashore or a mountain meadow. Imagine asking him or her a question and imagine that you can hear the response. Just as you would turn a radio dial to get static-free reception, keep subtly adjusting your inner dial until the image, sound, and sensation are well defined.

You may ask, "But isn't this just my imagination and not a real communication?" Actually, your imagination is the key to connect with inner realms and other dimensions—it's what unlocks your intuition. The more you practice this method, the less "static" you'll have in your mind, and the more accurate your ability to communicate will be.

Finding Your Rhythm

Have you ever visited a new place that made you instantly realize how homesick you were for it, even though you'd never been there before? This occurred for me the first time I visited Thailand. In that tropical country, I found a richness of the senses that fed a deep hunger within me that I wasn't even aware of until I arrived. The memory of that visit hangs humid and vibrant in the curves of my mind.

The night my plane landed in Thailand, I took a taxi to my hotel in the northern city of Chiang Mai. The taxi driver rapidly zigzagged through a jungle of thousands of motorbikes and cars. Whole families—children and parents holding bamboo baskets filled with chickens or other miscellaneous belongings—all clung tenuously to one single motorcycle. Somehow they tenaciously maintained their balance as they wove in and out of the traffic.

While I looked out the open window at the traffic, my senses were flooded with the intoxicating blend of sights and smells—from raw sewage to food being cooked by street-side vendors to the night-blooming flowers. Beneath it all, however, I could sense a pulse that seemed not only ancient but also wildly invigorating and modern. Every country has its own unique rhythm, and I was already beginning to get a feel for the cadence of this steamy country. I philosophically told myself that once I quit resisting and aligned with this frenetic energy of cars, trucks, rickshaws, and motorbikes, it wouldn't seem so chaotic and frightening to me.

Just as I entertained that thought, the taxi driver jerked the wheel, and the cab swerved into oncoming traffic. Although he wasn't going very fast, he managed to plow head-on into a motorcycle. The motor-cyclist and his passenger slid over the hood of our taxi, smashing against the windshield in what seemed like slow motion. Somehow they scrambled to get back on their motorcycle . . . and, unfazed by the jarring incident, kept on going . . . as did the taxi driver. I looked around in shock, but people on the sidewalks seemed to take it in stride. Suddenly I wasn't so sure that I wanted to get into the rhythm of this madness.

For the first few days in Chiang Mai, I was terrified of even crossing the street, since every rickshaw, taxi, car, and motorcycle seemed hell-bent on hitting me. (I was jet-lagged and a little out of sync with everything, including myself.) So even if it meant taking a longer route through the city, I did everything I could to avoid having to navigate from one side of the street to the other.

One evening, I could avoid it no longer: I was faced with the daunting task of traversing the busy street corner near the Night Bazaar. As there was no way around it, I took a few deep breaths and became very still within myself. Although the world was bus-tling around me, in my tranquility I began to harmonize with the underlying pulse of the place. It started small, like a faint tapping in the corner of my mind. Then, as the sound grew, a tendril of energy from my heart reached out to the center of the beat of life around me . . . I connected to it and felt it begin to resonate in my soul. Then my vibration and the pulsation of the city blended together inside of me.

With ease and grace, I stepped into the busy street. I didn't stop or hesitate or try to dodge cars—I just let the great sea of humanity and glut of vehicles flow around me. It was almost as if everything slowed down while I crossed the street and then sped back up once I was safely on the other side. I know this isn't what happened, but it felt that way. It felt like floating down a river and going with the current, as opposed to trying to swim up a river, constantly strug-gling against it.

Just as I was getting into the tempo of the city, I headed toward the mountains of northern Thailand, where I was to conduct a seminar. There, the pace slowed down considerably—in the quiet of the countryside, far from the noise and distractions of the city,

I began to sense and feel a slower and older rhythm than in the city. As each day passed, I could feel my spirit begin to merge and align with this ancient beat.

The room in which I taught my seminar was perched above a small creek, and below it we could see a mother elephant and her baby. Nearby we could also see a bamboo-roofed platform, which housed the young *mahout,* whose job it is to bond with and take care of the elephant for life. The mahout and his elephant almost never separate; in a sense, they become one another's family. During my seminar, I'd catch glimpses of the mahout gracefully draping his body over the baby elephant or tenderly offering the mama elephant bananas. I could sense how the rhythm of these relationships was connected to the larger rhythm of the land . . . languid, liquid, and timeless.

I believe that elephants embody the soul of Thailand, and I gained an even deeper understanding of this when I had the opportunity to ride one of these splendid mammoths. At first I felt tense and off balance because I was riding bareback—my legs straddled the creature's neck, my bare feet pressed against his shoulders, and my hands grasped the top of his head. As the elephant climbed up and down the riverbanks, my body was wrenched forward and back. I felt unstable and was afraid that I was going to fall onto the sharp rocks below. Then I slowly allowed myself to let go of my fears and enter into the energy of the elephant—and instantly, my body relaxed. I could feel the creature's powerful muscles ripple beneath my body as we ambled across the creeks and into the teak forest. I'd always thought of elephant skin as tough and thick, but beneath my hands it felt supple and sensitive. In fact, a fly landed on the elephant's head at one point, and he immediately swished his ears to chase it off. I realized that his hide was delicate enough to sense even the presence of a small insect.

Once I let go and connected with the spirit of the elephant, everything seemed to slow down. During my ride, my breath became unhurried and a quiet joy filled me. I don't know how to explain it, but it was as if the world around me was going at a more deliberate and leisurely pace. The ripples in the stream seemed sensuously fluid, and the birds flying overhead seemed to flap their wings in slow motion. I realized that I'd entered into the rhythm of the elephant and was seeing the world through his eyes. Even after I was off his back, the pace stayed with me . . . it took more than an hour before everything returned to normal speed for me.

Once I returned to the ordinary pace of humans, I proceeded with one of the purposes of my trip. Since my seminar took place right after the large tsunami hit Thailand's shores, I wanted to do something to help the survivors of the devastation and decided that a ceremony for the land, the victims, and everyone touched by the disaster might be beneficial. So the seminar participants and I created a moving and beautiful ceremony, choosing to use water as a vehicle for our prayers because it holds the energetic pattern of sound. Substantial research by scientists in Japan has proven that water retains energy—for example, if it's prayed over and then frozen, the subsequent crystals are symmetrical and beautiful. But if it's been shouted at in anger and then frozen, the crystals that form when frozen are uneven and unsightly in appearance.

I'd been inspired by the scientific research of Masaru Emoto, which is contained in his groundbreaking book *The Hidden Messages in Water*. Mr. Emoto performed thousands of scientific experiments in which he exposed water to different words and various kinds of music, and then he froze the water and photographed the crystals that formed. What he found, over and over, was that the vibration of positive words caused beautiful crystals to form in the water, while the vibration of negative words caused the crystals to either not form at all or to be deformed.

With these findings in mind, each seminar participant and I put our prayers and blessings into small amounts of water and poured them into a nearby mountain stream. One woman from China provided water that had been blessed by 100 Buddhist monks, while a participant from Australia brought water that had been collected from several sacred sites around the world—from the Ganges to Lourdes. We intended that the energy, love, and prayers we put into the water would travel from the stream out into the sea, and eventually be subtly felt on the far shores of Thailand, Sri Lanka, and the other island nations touched by the disaster.

As part of our ceremony, we also floated traditional Thai offerings of flowers, candles, and incense in the stream, and it was a beautiful sight to watch them bounce and float on the water. At the conclusion of the ceremony, we lit and released a huge "fire balloon" (a large rice-paper bag that has a fire built inside it). The heat from the fire carried the balloon high into the sky where it hovered and glowed, and we hoped that it would take our prayers into the heavens and then release them to those left behind. We intended that the uplifting vibration created by our prayers would, in our own small way, help ease some of the suffering and contribute to the restoration of the natural rhythm of the land that had been so devastated by the tsunami.

BALANCE AND THE BEAT

I believe that everything, no matter if it's animate and inanimate, has a rhythm. When we're in harmony with these rhythms, life is in balance. When our life is in disarray, it's usually because we're out of sync with our own internal and external cadence.

You can create balance in your life when you take the time to discover your own beat. Once you've found it, you can then expand your awareness to merge your inner pace with the pace of the world around you. By doing so, you can begin to experience the precious pulse of life itself.

The way to discover the rhythm of an object or person is to first become very still. Imagine that there's a tempo emanating from it, and then visualize what it would feel like to synchronize your internal vibration with the energy of that other beat. This practice will allow you to connect intimately on an energetic level with any object. (This is similar to listening to a band and then tapping your foot to the beat.) Native people once used a very similar method to "communicate" with plants, animals, and stones—they'd listen for its inner rhythm, and then they'd imagine harmonizing with that rhythmic vibration in order to enter the item's consciousness and "hear" its voice.

STEPS TO EMPOWERMENT

Learning how to be in harmony with the underlying rhythms of the world around you—no matter where you are—is one of the secrets to inner peace. Here's an exercise that you can do to help you achieve this:

> *Choose one object that you want to connect with, and then close your eyes and visualize it in front of you. Pretend that it's making a rhythmic sound. Now imagine that you're attuning to the sound the same way that you'd match the movement of a dance partner or tap your feet to the music you hear on the radio. As you do so, notice if you're aware of any messages or feelings emanating from the object.*

The more you practice this exercise, the more you'll be able to connect to the consciousness of the world around you.

Your Spirit
Is Nurtured
by the Truth

During my time with Aboriginal elders in Australia, I was taken to the bush to discover my animal clan—this is the creature spirit that oversees a unified group of people. (The practice of belonging to an animal clan is common in almost all native cultures, and I wrote about this experience in greater detail in my autobiography, *If I Can Forgive, So Can You*).

My experience in the bushlands allowed me to discovered that I was in the crow clan. Afterward, the elders stressed to me the importance of finding my individual spirit animal as well. You see, individuals within each clan also have their own personal animal ally. For example, in Native American tradition the people in one village might all belong to the bear clan. However, each person might have a different spirit animal, such as a deer, badger, or fox.

Spirit animals have many other names, such as *animal totems, power animals,* or *animal allies,* and they connect individuals more deeply to their own nature. To discover my Aboriginal animal ally, I was taken deep into a cave that went straight down into the earth. While in the bright Australian sunshine, I'd been excited by the prospect of discovering my spirit animal . . . but as I started my climb deep down into the darkness, I was scared. I found it difficult to maneuver through the narrow crevices, and I was afraid of falling as the rocks crumbled beneath my feet. As I descended the steep cliff into even darker blackness, the air entering my lungs became colder and more piercing.

Once I reached the flat bottom of the cave, I was given a belt of tightly braided Aboriginal hair to wear around my waist for protection. (Native tradition dictates that whenever one travels to the inner realms, it's prudent to wear some kind of talisman to protect against the so-called dark forces that may enter the body during the journey.) I was then instructed to get down on the ground, stretch my body out on a flat rock, and close my eyes. I felt sick to my stomach and wanted to leave. The walls felt as if they might collapse on top of me, and I just didn't feel right, but I forced myself to think about this experience as the opportunity of a lifetime, reminding myself how lucky I was to be there.

As I lay on my back on the cold stone slab, my body began to shiver. The air was damp and musty. Chilly whiffs of a moldy, fetid odor entered my nostrils—it was as if something had fallen into the cave, crawled into a crevice, and died. I could make out the faint glow of light from the opening overhead, but down in the bowels of the cave, it was so dark that it was difficult to see anything around me.

Without my sense of sight to give me perspective, I had a heightened awareness of the booming sounds coming from the didgeridoo that the elders began to play. Its eerie music haunted the icy air around me, and wisps of its vibration seemed to reach out to touch me. At first the sound seemed to linger lightly on my skin, but then it began to steadily penetrate inside of me, the way water seeps through sand. This hypnotic resonance made me sleepier and sleepier . . . at some point I dozed off and drifted into a dream state.

I found myself on a sunny rock where everything was bright green, and I didn't know where I was. I felt much smaller than usual, yet it didn't seem abnormal that I wasn't my usual size; in fact, none of what surrounded me seemed unfamiliar. As I looked up at a large leaf above me, I realized that the sunlight shining through it was bathing everything underneath—including my tiny body—in a greenish light. I then peered down at my feet and observed that they'd transformed into claws; when I examined my arms, they appeared to be full of scales. Yet none of this seemed strange to me. I pushed up and down a few times on my forelegs, feeling alert and focused. Cocking my head from side to side, I surveyed my surroundings and enjoyed the feeling of warmth radiating from the rock below me.

In a remote part of my mind, I remember thinking *Wow! Cool—I'm a lizard!* Although I must have realized that I was dreaming, it all seemed so real. I then remembered that a Native American teacher of mine had once told me that he could turn himself into a fox, and I realized that this must have been what he meant. *Maybe this is what he called shape-shifting,* I thought. As a lizard, I experienced the world from a different mind-set; altering my shape had shifted my perspective. I saw things in terms of heat and cold and felt very happy simply because I was soaking up the sun on a warm rock.

Then all those lizardlike sensations abruptly disappeared, and something inside of me changed. I felt an intense and dark force winding its way through my body, like a sidewinder writhing back and forth inside my abdomen, and I couldn't stop it. Then, just as quickly as it entered, it slithered out of me. It didn't feel evil—just powerful and wild. I wasn't sure what was going on, but the experience frightened me tremendously.

I don't know how long I was dreaming. When the didgeridoo unexpectedly ceased, I opened my eyes and returned to my own body. I was lying on the ground and felt even colder than before I'd fallen asleep—in fact, my body was shaking uncontrollably from the chill. The sun position above must have changed slightly while I was "dreaming" because a ray of sun had encroached upon the darkness, creating an amber glow on the ceiling of the upper cave. I could barely make out faint shapes as I sat up and looked around, and I felt dizzy and unwell.

The elders surrounded me and asked what animal I became. I shakily answered, "I was some kind of lizard." I didn't want to talk about it, though . . . I just wanted to leave. It took great effort on my part not to cut the process short. I knew that it was the kind of experience that people yearned for, so I denied my body's gut reaction and convinced myself to stay longer in order to keep sharing my dream.

The Aborigines asked questions about the color and shape of the lizard until they could determine exactly what kind I'd become. I could tell from their expressions that they hadn't expected this to be my animal ally. I was later told that they had believed I'd become some kind of bird that lived in the bush. I didn't quite understand: *Was it better to be a bush hen than a lizard?* Even after I climbed back up onto level ground and into the warm light of the Australian sun, I felt faint. Nevertheless, I told myself to be grateful for the spiritual experience that had occurred.

CONFRONT YOUR TRUE FEELINGS

Connecting to an animal ally in the seclusion of an underground cave may sound exotic and even spiritually thrilling, but the experience wasn't at all glamorous. Afterward, I felt disoriented and unclean, and every time I thought about the cave, I'd become sick. During my dream I'd felt as if something foreign had entered me without my permission, and I was very unsettled about it.

Whenever I told people what had happened, I convinced them—and myself—that it was an amazing spiritual experience. I denied the truth about the situation, which was that it was upsetting and disturbing. I described what I'd *wanted* to feel rather than what I'd *actually* felt. It worked for a while . . . I even started to feel as if my experience had been a positive one.

Unfortunately, the problem with not telling ourselves the truth is that this approach takes its toll on the soul over time. This denial of the truth not only erodes the spirit, it can have harmful consequences on the body as well. So often we have experiences that disappoint, trouble, or embarrass us, yet we blindly deny the truth of the matter. By suggesting that these events were wondrous, loving, adventurous, or remarkable—when in truth they were not—is incredibly damaging to our psyche.

Perhaps you know some people who work hard to appear to be enjoying a perfect marriage, living an effortless lifestyle, or working at a phenomenal job. Nevertheless, you can tell that beneath the surface, they're suffering. If they're not confronting their true feelings about their situation, they may succeed in making it look great to everyone else, but they're actually harming themselves.

Keep in mind that lying to others about your situation diminishes your self-esteem, *but lying to yourself damages your soul.* The soul loves the truth. Even when it's hard to face, it's healing to be able to look at your life with stark honesty.

When I confronted my own feelings about my experience in the cave, I found that the reality was that I was extremely uncomfortable there. I finally admitted to myself that I felt guilty about disliking what had occurred because I'd really *wanted* it to be a profound spiritual experience. When I started being honest with myself about it, I realized that my experience *wasn't* spiritual—it was frightening and unnerving. Once I arrived at this understanding, I was able to revisit my memory of the experience with candor. This acknowledgment of the truth made me feel stronger, clearer, and more empowered as a result. My fear of the sidewinding darkness melted in the healing light of the truth.

STEPS TO EMPOWERMENT

Is there a situation in your life that you're not being honest with yourself about? Are you in a relationship that looks ideal to everyone else, for instance, but isn't actually that great? Or have you ever been at a party, concert, gathering, or vacation and found that you're trying to convince yourself that you're having a great time, but you really aren't? You might have thought, *Who wouldn't enjoy themselves in this situation, or with this person?* Well, if the truth is that *you* aren't enjoying it and you *are* miserable, don't try to deny it . . . embrace it.

Ask yourself what you're afraid it will cost you if you admit what you're actual feeling—after all, a difficult situation can't be remedied unless you admit that there's a problem. The first step to authenticity is to let go of what you think you should feel or what others expect of you. Then, in a forthright manner, admit to yourself the reality of your state of affairs. It may not be easy, but it *is* essential.

Keep in mind that what you tell others is less important than what you tell yourself, so start first by telling the truth to yourself. This practice might seem difficult in the beginning, but once you go for it, you'll find that it becomes easier to admit it to others, too.

After a while it may feel so liberating to be honest with yourself that you become addicted to it! Yet the most beneficial outcome of this candor is that the situations you find yourself in will have more meaning and will be more rewarding for you.

Discovering
Your Spirit Animals

During my harrowing experience down in an Australian cave to find my animal totem, I was surprised to find that my ally was a lizard. Although I've always had an affinity for reptiles (as well as a number of other creatures), the animal that I feel most closely aligned with is the black panther, and I've known for a very long time that it's my spirit animal. I don't know why the panther didn't appear in Australia—perhaps because it isn't a native animal of the "Land Down Under," and the Aborigines expected that my ally would be one of the creatures of their land.

The most remarkable thing about this experience, however, wasn't what happened to me in the cave, but what occurred at exactly the same time in Seattle, which was my home at the time. When I returned from my trip, I had a frantic call on my answering machine. It was from a woman whom I didn't know very well, but who'd attended a few of my seminars, and all the message said was, "Denise, it's really important—I have to see you."

She came over the next day and told me that she'd had a very disturbing dream where she was down in a cave and it was very cold. Dark-skinned people had surrounded her and told her that she was going to find her animal totem. Then she'd suddenly found herself turning into a black panther, leaping up from rock to rock, until she finally sprang out of the cave and raced across the plain.

The woman said that this was no ordinary dream—it seemed too real. She was particularly distressed by the fact that when she woke up, her shoulders were sore as if from strenuous exercise . . .

and her hands were as raw as if she'd used them to really run across rocks and sand. She showed them to me, and they did indeed look as if they'd been rubbed with sandpaper.

She said that she knew that she was meant to tell me about the dream. Although she didn't see me in her vision, she'd somehow felt my presence with her. I didn't know what to make of her experience, but I found it extraordinary that it had occurred at *exactly* the same time that I was in the cave in Australia. (It was also curious that she'd become a panther, especially since she didn't have any affinity for this animal.) While one part of my consciousness was with the Aborigines in the cave, perhaps another part of me—guided by the sound of the didgeridoo—subconsciously journeyed to my true animal totem, and for some inexplicable reason, the woman from my seminar came along with me. Whatever the explanation, this experience was one more confirmation of the mysterious realities of the inner planes and the power of animal totems.

FINDING YOUR SPIRIT ALLIES

There's a place beyond this realm that's as real and vibrant as anything you can experience here on earth. It's where mystics, shamans, and medicine men or women travel to gain wisdom and understanding about the events of our world . . . and it's also available to you. By simply being still and meditating, you can begin to gain entrance into this dimension. There are many things that you can discover by entering into these invisible realms—one of the most powerful is your individual spirit animal because your totem can help activate many beneficial qualities within you.

For many years I lead ten-day vision quests (see my book *Quest*), and the most powerful and moving experience was often the discovery of power animals. Once they're discovered, the animals' beneficial qualities begin to impact people's lives. For example, if someone has the horse for his or her spirit animal, then "horse qualities" of freedom, strength, and power grow within that person over time.

I've found that when I connect with my spirit panther, I go at a slower and more relaxed pace in life. Panther energy helps me be active when I need to be, but also helps me fully relax at other times. (I'll admit that I identify with a panther's inclination toward long, leisurely naps between times of activity.) And my spirit animal brings a sensuous enjoyment into my life, especially when I become very busy and forget to make time for being quiet and restful.

In order to find your animal ally, you don't have to do it the hard way like I did. You don't have to travel to faraway lands or endure the cold, uncomfortable, and scary domain of an underground cave. You can access your spirit animal safely, using simple ways that avoid pain or fear—and the magical awareness you gain will make the journey all the more worthwhile.

Steps to Empowerment

There are several ways to discover your totems—the easiest is to begin to watch repetitive signs around you in everyday reality. To utilize this method, the first step is to ask Spirit to give you a sign. You might say, "Creator, please give me a sign that will let me know my totem." Then begin to notice any animals that continually show up around you. If you see the same one appearing again and again in an unusual way or over a short period of time (such as the actual animal; a symbol for it, such as a statue or figurine; or mention of it in a book, photograph, or song), then there's a good chance that this is your totem. This repetitive appearance can also mean that the spirit of that particular animal wants to connect with you and is trying to give you a message. In other words, your spirit animal is using its physical counterpart to project important information to you.

Pay particular attention when an animal appears to you, especially if it comes into your awareness at least three times in a short period. When this occurs, take a moment to be still and ask yourself what the message is. For example, if you turn on the radio and the announcer is talking about the migration habits of bears and then later you pass a billboard with a smiling bear on it, this might be a sign. But if you stroll down the aisle at the grocery store, glance over and spy a row of honey bears smiling down at you, and then have a dream about bears that very night, then it's time to really begin to listen to the signs. And if bears continue to come into your awareness again and again, especially after you've asked for a sign about your totem, then there's a good chance that the bear is your spirit animal. When this occurs, it's important to meditate on these appearances to begin to understand what the meaning is for you.

Spirit animals may also show up in your dreams, visions, or meditations. A way to find your animal ally is to relax, close your eyes, and imagine that you're going to a special place in nature—it might be a meadow, a cave, or a mountaintop—to meet your ally. While you're very relaxed, ask yourself this question: *If I knew what my totem was, what would it be?* Then use your imagination to visualize this animal approaching you. Although this technique sounds simplistic, it can in fact be very profound.

Once you discover your totem using this technique, the positive qualities of that animal manifest within you and begin to be revealed outside of you. For example, if you discover that yours is an eagle, you'll find that the qualities of strength, clarity, and being able to see a situation from afar will begin to develop within you. Discovering your totem and communing with it will then start to deepen your connection with the natural world and enrich your life's experience in profound ways.

The Power
of Forgiveness

There's a lull that occurs between the moment a traumatic event has occurred for a loved one and the moment you hear of it. Although in your soul you already know what's happened and have begun to mourn, the conscious part of you continues to experience life as usual for a little bit longer. Yet there's an imperceptible but tangible shift of awareness that occurs in between those two times—to me, it feels like the seconds between when you lose your balance and the instant you hit the ground. Even as you free-fall, you know in a moment that you're going to eventually crash.

You can sense this subtle shift of energy precisely before you answer the late-night call with the news that changes your life forever. When the call came with the report about my father, for instance, I denied what my soul already knew was true.

"Denise, your dad is dying. Come back as soon as you can," one of my father's neighbors said urgently. I held the phone away from my ear and stared at it numbly. I couldn't believe what I'd just heard. My dad had colon cancer, but I hadn't expected to receive that call so soon. Actually, I didn't expect to *ever* receive it. Even though he no longer played a big part in my daily life, somehow I thought he'd always be around.

Shaking myself out of my stupor, I immediately threw some clothes into a suitcase that was already partially packed. As I raced to the airport, I wondered if I'd subconsciously known that I'd need to be prepared even if I couldn't consciously face that truth.

At the terminal, I was told that it would take three flights to get from where I was teaching in central California to the small

Oregon town where my father and his second wife lived. The first flight was bumpy, but I barely noticed the turbulence because my thoughts were far away. I leaned my head against the window and thought about my relationship with the man who was my father. We'd never been very close, especially after the sexual abuse that had occurred during my childhood.

The emotional scars and the shame of what he had done to me night after night in his bed when I was a little girl—while my mother was in a mental hospital—were still fresh. Even though it had occurred 40 years earlier, I could not forget that abuse. Yet despite those memories, I not only visited him many times over the years, but I also tried to establish deeper ties with him. Regardless of the open wounds from my childhood, I continued to yearn for a loving father-daughter relationship with him. As I sat on the plane to go see him, I feared that it may have been too late for that.

While the plane bounced around in the sky, I thought back on the two times I'd tried to talk to my father about what had occurred when I was a child. Both times he denied it and ended the conversation quickly by abruptly walking out of the room. Once I asked him if he thought that I'd made it up—somehow it was important to me to know what he felt. He didn't answer me, so I asked him again, "Do you think I'm lying?" Again, he didn't answer me but merely looked down at the floor. I suppose that was the closest I ever got to an apology.

After those failed attempts at coming to a resolution, we tried to carry on with an unspoken pact of silence. Nevertheless, the abuse suffused my awareness whenever I was with him—it was an invisible, but nonetheless rock-solid, wall that stood between us. Even when I wasn't thinking about it, my body reacted differently when I was around him. For example, just one of his most innocent little half hugs would cause a wave of nausea to unexpectedly wash over me.

The emotional pain from the abuse just would not heal. I didn't need to consciously think about the past in order for it to be there—it always lurked buried beneath the surface of my psyche, ready to uncoil and strike out at any moment. Despite how irrational it might have been, I continued to think that if only my father would admit what had happened and apologize for it, then my pain would go away and my wounds would instantly heal. I still strove for that ideal, even as I rode on the plane to my father's deathbed . . . maybe it wasn't too late! I had crazy visions of an apology and reconciliation, even if it came in the final moments of his life.

I finally touched down at the small local airport in my father's town. A family member picked me up, and by the look on her face, I could tell that the news wasn't good. Indeed, she said, "I'm so sorry, Denise. You're too late—he died a few hours ago."

Her words didn't register at first. I couldn't quite believe that he wasn't alive anymore. "He can't be dead," I stated. "Where's his body? I want to see it."

"You can't. We've sent it to be cremated."

"If he's not cremated yet, then I can still go see it," I said adamantly. I didn't know why I wanted to see his body, but somehow it seemed important.

After much discussion back at his home, it was finally agreed that I could go see my father's body, which was being held in a warehouse-type building in the industrial area of town. When I arrived there, a troll-looking man behind the front desk scrutinized me with squinty eyes.

"I'm here to see the body of my father," I announced.

With the tone of authority bestowed upon people who have small jobs and like to feel important, he informed me that it wouldn't be possible.

"I *will* see my father's body," I quietly demanded, as I gave him a hard, penetrating look.

My obstinate determination seemed to shake him for a moment, but he recovered and said haughtily, "Okay, but don't say I didn't warn you."

I was escorted into a harshly lit and cold room, where it became clear why the troll at the front desk didn't want me to go in: My father, gray and lifeless, lay on a slab, and while he was partially covered with a sheet, his head and the exposed parts of his body were badly bruised. He didn't die of head injuries, but there were gashes and nicks on his head and face. He was a big man, and I think that he must have been difficult to carry—they must have dropped him several times while getting him into the warehouse.

I pulled up a crate and sat down next to him. For a while I just sat there . . . and then I reached up and put my hand in his. It was cold and yet strangely comforting. It was the first time I could remember that my stomach didn't tighten when we touched.

I started to talk out loud. I didn't care if anyone else heard me—I had a lot to get off my chest. "I'm so damn angry at you! Now that you're dead, you're never going to admit to abusing me. You're never going to apologize for what you did! And I'm mad that you died before this could be healed," I said, trembling as I spoke.

I was crying so hard that I was having trouble getting the words out, but I continued, "I don't even know why I'm saying this now, because I'm not even sure that I believe it, but I forgive you. I forgive you for taking advantage of me when I was small. I forgive you for the way you put Mother in the mental hospital. I forgive you for ignoring me when I was shot and for not helping me when I was struggling to try to get in to college.

"I forgive you for telling me 'Good luck' when I called you and said that I needed to borrow some money to fix the hole in my aorta, even when I told you I'd die without surgery. But damn it! I forgive you for that, too!" I was shouting and not thinking rationally. Everything that I'd stored up for years erupted out of me, and although I was saying words of forgiveness, I didn't feel as if I were actually forgiving him because I was becoming more and more enraged. A lifetime of anger bubbled to the surface as I continued to list all the things I "forgave" him for.

Then I heard these words, *which seemed to come from my dad*: "All those years *you* kept hoping that I'd come forward to ask for your forgiveness, *I* kept hoping that you'd come forward and forgive me."

Suddenly the anger and sadness dropped away. My father was dead, but I'd heard his words almost as clearly as if he were still alive, and all of my anguish disappeared. I felt devoid of emotion; I was completely empty as I realized that all those years I'd been waiting for an apology, *he'd* been waiting for my forgiveness.

I had to take the first step . . . it had to start with me! In that moment, I let go of the resentment and anger I'd harbored for a lifetime. I just surrendered, and it drained out of me—I didn't have to hold on to any of it anymore. A sense of salvation and freedom filled me, as the room overflowed with the same shimmering golden light I'd experienced when I was shot at age 17. As I squeezed the father's hand tightly, it didn't feel cold anymore—I knew that I loved him and that he loved me. Wonderful forgotten memories from childhood flooded my being—of my father fixing the tire on my red bicycle, the day he pulled all of us through the snow on an old wooden sled, and how he used to toss my little two-year-old brother, Brand, into the air as he squealed with delight. I loved my dad . . . I really loved him.

I stood up and fully looked at him. For the first time I could remember, I really saw my father. In the past, I'd usually avoid looking into his eyes—but as I looked at him in that moment, I became aware of the pain and disappointment that had plagued him during his life. I sensed his self-disgust for abusing his daughter, and I saw all of his unfulfilled dreams and heartaches. And I wept for him for the first time in my life.

Gently stroking his forehead, I said, "Good-bye, Father." I hadn't called him "Father" since I was a kid—I always called him by his first name, Dick, as it had seemed more appropriate. Now I was saying good-bye to Dick. I was saying good-bye to my father.

The lightness I experienced stayed with me long after I left the warehouse. Even at the memorial service we had a few weeks later, I felt joyous about the opportunity to celebrate Father's life. We created a "stage," told great stories about his life, and shared photos. It was the first time that my siblings—Heather, Gordon, and Brand—and I had been together since we were children, and it felt like a kind of homecoming. Later we stood together outside to cherish the enormous rainbow that splashed across the sky. Even though it was a sad event, there was a lot of joy and love shared.

INITIATE A CYCLE OF LOVE

No matter what others have done to you, it's possible to forgive them. And it's immensely important to do so . . . not for them, but for you. Although you can't erase your past, you *can* heal from any residual wounds. The first step is to acknowledge that someone else has negatively impacted you. It's all right to hold people accountable for their acts and feel angry because you need to honor and accept how you feel about them and the situation. This is what occurred when I was yelling at my dead father's body—I was telling the truth about what I felt, and it was extremely healing.

The next step is real forgiveness. This can help you release anger, bitterness, and resentment—all the emotions that can eat away at you over time if you let them—and allow you to get on with your life instead of nursing old wounds. It's human to want to penalize those who've wronged you, yet no amount of punishment for those who hurt you will ever help you heal. In fact, the anger that you cling to only serves to damage you, not them.

Forgiveness is something that you do for *your* sake and *your* healing. You forgive in order to gain inner peace, joy, and serenity for yourself, not necessarily for the people who wronged you. Some individuals hold on to their resentment because they have a subconscious belief that sooner or later their nemesis will apologize or "make it up" to them, just as I was hoping my father would do on his deathbed. Well, the truth may be that if they haven't done it by now, they probably never will. You might never be able to "even the score." Those who wronged you may never change . . . and even if they did, would it really alleviate your pain over the injustice that you've suffered?

Avoid the temptation to hold on to resentment and hatred—stop using it as justification to continue acting like a victim. Don't let your perpetrators become your excuse for not living the life you desire, and don't blame them for everything that's wrong in your world. Granting clemency means being willing to grab life by the reins and take your power back.

This doesn't mean that you need to forget, absolve, or condone the actions of another. But while you may never be able to forgive someone's deeds, there's tremendous value in forgiving the individual who committed them. Understanding that each person's actions are dictated by his or her conditioning makes it easier to forgive. Everyone has a reason for doing what they do, and often that reason comes out of fear. Even if, in retrospect, a person could see another way to act, they responded as well as they could in that moment given their fear, their early-childhood conditioning, and the influence of their culture. It's valuable to understand why people act the way they do, but it's also helpful to acknowledge the reality of what they are—which means admitting that they may have the capacity to commit hurtful acts again.

Now, forgiveness doesn't mean that you need to become that person's best friend. Understanding why someone acts the way they do—and acknowledging the truth of the situation—can be enough to begin the healing for you. Of course, it can be extremely difficult and is usually an ongoing process; that is, it's not an absolute, one-time decision. It isn't an act . . . it's a context . . . and it can't be forced. It isn't as easy as blithely deciding, "Okay, right now I'm forgiving that person who harmed me."

You'll find that trying to make a unilateral declaration of forgiveness usually doesn't work—and listing everyone you want to absolve and then ticking off each name as you try to pardon them one by one doesn't work either. It's important to know that the way to forgiveness can take time, and it can deepen as a result of honestly exploring the roots of your past and then gaining an understanding of the forces at play in the situation.

It's vital that you have patience with yourself. There may be some days when you feel completely free of past resentments, while there may be others when they seem to well up again. Sometimes feigning forgiveness can be a means of negating your anger before you're ready to release it—it's important to honor the process and allow yourself to be where you are, even as you hold an intention for true forgiveness to occur.

Sometimes forgiveness can be interactive and sometimes it can't. Talking to those for whom you harbor bitterness can sometimes be helpful, but not everyone is going to be receptive to communication. In fact, the initial attempts to express yourself may be extremely difficult and fall short of your expectations. But don't lose faith—if you talk from your heart and speak your truth, your words will act like seeds that take root and grow over time. (When you're unable to heal through communication, or if the person with whom you're angry is dead, it's still valuable to reach into inner realms to find resolve and peace.)

Also, know that what you put into motion now with your willingness to forgive can positively impact later generations. When you truly cross the threshold to forgiveness, you break the cycle and the negative patterns of abuse, ridicule, betrayal, rejection, discouragement, cruelty, abandonment, lack of love, failure, or scorn that may otherwise be doomed to continue for years. Be the one to initiate a new cycle of love, support, and kindness that will follow you for generations to come.

STEPS TO EMPOWERMENT

To begin your own process of healing, make a list of the people and situations that you haven't forgiven. Then, as a starting point, choose one from your list that will be the easiest to forgive. Once your selection is made, take some time to acknowledge what you really feel about this person or situation, and write it all out . . . all of it. What's the stark truth?

Next, as hard as it may seem, take a moment to see the world through that person's eyes—imagine how the situations you were both involved in might have felt like for him or her. As difficult as this can be to do, it's important to understand that even if this individual did do something horrible to you, he or she did the best he or she could at the time. You don't need to agree with that person about what happened, and you're by no means justifying it—you're just attempting to understand what motivated it. The final step in the healing process is to actively forgive him or her. Remember that you don't need to forgive the deed (some deeds may in fact be unforgivable), but it's important to forgive the person.

Once you've successfully forgiven and begin to feel the healing results, repeat this exercise with the other people on your list.

Realize What's
Important in Life

L iving in the country, I find that the energy of the land seeps into my dreams at night as well as during the day. Over time I've been able to connect more deeply to the planet since moving from the city to the country—my dreams have become more vivid and rich, as if the land trusts me and speaks to me in the images that fill my night hours.

For example, on September 11, 2001, at 5 A.M. Pacific Standard Time, I was awakened by a frightening nightmare. In it I saw an enormous tree that was hundreds of feet wide and so high that I couldn't see the top of it, and it was being chopped down by a fanatical bearded man standing at the tree's base. A woman screamed as she tried to get away by climbing high up it—suddenly the tree collapsed into itself and there was blood everywhere. I woke up crying and trembling with fright, and my heart was pounding so hard that I could hardly breathe.

It was just before dawn and the sky was starting to brighten, so I walked outside in my nightgown and tried to dispel the disturbing images with the crispness of the morning air. I'd never had a dream like that before, and I needed to eradicate it from my memory. I got in my car and drove to the top of Summer Hill (the tall hill behind our home). As I got out and walked through the tall grasses, morning dew dampened the bottom of my thin gown. I hugged my arms around my waist and stood waiting for the sun to rise from behind the far mountains.

That nightmare had been one of the most terrifying ones I'd ever had. *What could it mean?* I wondered. *Was some deep part of my unexplored psyche rising to the surface to be examined?* And then, as the first ray of light pierced the sky, I heard an inner voice say, "It begins today."

What begins today? I was confused. Still upset about my dream, I couldn't make sense of this message. I headed back to the car, asking myself over and over, *What is it that begins today?*

I tried to put those disturbing feelings and questions out of my mind as I drove down the hill toward the house. Once inside, I made myself a cup of green tea. I was standing in the kitchen, cradling the warm mug in my hands to ward off the chill, when a friend from Kansas called. We chatted for a few minutes, and then she broke in with, "Denise, wait a minute. There's something on TV I need to look at."

A minute later she came back to the phone and cried, "Oh my God! The northern tower of the World Trade Center in New York City has been hit!"

Appalled by what had occurred, we continued to talk. Since I don't have a TV, she kept giving me updates as she monitored her set. When I heard that a plane had hit the second tower as well, I was shell-shocked and unable to speak. I thought of my nightmare *that had taken place just before the planes crashed:* In it, a tree as large as one of the twin towers had collapsed in on itself. And as unimaginable images filled the airwaves, I kept remembering similar images of terror that I'd witnessed in my nightmare—the bearded man, the woman frantically climbing for her life, the screams, and the massive amount of blood—it was so terrifying that all I could do was weep.

"IT BEGINS TODAY"

Since that morning, I've asked myself many times what the words meant that came to me on Summer Hill that fateful morning: "It begins today." Perhaps it signified that 9/11 was a pivotal event and the beginning of a new and alarming era in our history, or maybe it foreshadowed our entering into a new cycle of the earth. As much as modern life alienates us from nature, I don't believe that we can continue to separate ourselves from the planet where we live without dire consequences. The fate of humanity and the fate of the natural world are interwoven—the energy of the earth affects us just as we, in turn, affect it. The environment is being systematically destroyed through pollution and mismanagement of resources—so, as some have suggested, September 11, 2001, may also have signified the beginning of a massive life-and-death struggle for the destiny of our planet.

But perhaps my cryptic internal message was more personal. Maybe it means that it's important to put life in perspective and discover what's truly important and authentic. Once this is established, then it might be necessary to have the courage to step forward into the future with love and determination, no matter what's occurring.

On my personal journey through life, with all of its ups and downs, the most important lesson that I've learned is the value of joy. I believe that it's essential to create happiness for ourselves and then share it with as many people as we can. Maybe one of the messages from 9/11 is that joy becomes even more important in the face of adversity and struggle.

I believe that individual consciousness affects the mass consciousness, and one person who lives joyfully, without fear or distrust, can affect a multitude of people. Perhaps it will only be when the mass consciousness is motivated by joy rather than by fear that a gentler time can return to our planet.

Steps to Empowerment

What's something that you can do today that can motivate you toward joy? Is there an area of your life that's motivated by fear? If so, can you think of one step—it doesn't have to be big—that you could take today to move away from that fear and toward joy?

Each person, no matter what his or her life circumstances are, can make a difference, and it *does* start today. It's been said that "we were made for these times," and it's true—each one of us is here at a pivotal juncture in our planet's history. It can start with the single act of deciding what's truly important in life. Then slowly but deliberately, start to diminish what's trivial and expand what's essential. Dedicate your time to the things that nurture your soul.

For example, if you spend more time mowing your lawn and keeping up your flower beds than playing with your children, it may be time to adjust your priorities. If you know that your kids are a higher value to you than your yard, consider letting the grass just get a little higher and the garden a bit more overgrown. Don't postpone these decisions—implement them today. If you've wanted to give your time to a charity but keep getting distracted by other things on your agenda, find a way to prioritize your contributions to others and stop procrastinating.

Decide what's most important in your life and embrace it. Start spreading your wings, sharing your soul, and living your life to the fullest. Don't wait until you have more time, more skill, or more opportunity—don't stall. Do it now . . . let living begin *today.*

CONCLUSION

I woke up this morning and thought that I could smell the future. It was fresh and crisp like the air in springtime, but with a tinge of smoke, similar to the smell of our neighbor burning his grass before cultivating his vineyards.

The scent gave me a sense of expectation, and a feeling of trepidation at the same time—like the shadow of a cloud passing overhead that momentarily blots out the light on a sunny day. I don't know if this was the global future that I sensed, but it seemed to stretch far beyond my personal boundaries and into the world at large. I guess I'll have to wait and see what the days ahead hold . . . but in the meantime, I'm spending time breathing the country air, putting my roots into the earth, and watching for the messages that are revealed in the natural world around me.

I've learned so much in my life, and I cherish it all. Even though being shot when I was 17 took a terrible toll on me, I was fortunate because it offered me the joy of being embraced by the light. In those few moments beyond death's door, it was as if the Creator absorbed my essence, and I dissolved into that fluid love. My time in that realm taught me that we're each immortal beings, infinite and forever, and there is no death . . . only change. While the body we inhabit is born and dies, in truth *we* are never born or die.

I know now that everything—and I mean everything—is alive and filled with Spirit. Divine love is everywhere, and it's always expanding and renewing. God is truly omnipotent, and it's through a greater exploration of this planet and of our own life that we'll find Spirit in every possible crevice we search.

During my time in the land of golden light, I discovered absolute happiness that I can still access today, because I *know* that there is no separation between us and everything else. In essence, we are one—we're merged with the Source that dwells inside every living thing. I now comprehend that we're each a blessing, whether we believe it or think we deserve it or not.

Although there are times that my life that I do forget this, deep inside at the core of my being I always know the truth. I know that life isn't an accident, although I may find *myself* in an accident or two along the way. Making so-called mistakes is part of growing. Every experience in my life has given me a reminder of who I am—of who we all are—and that is Divine. ॐ~

Acknowledgments

I am immensely grateful, as always, to my daughter, Meadow, for her insights, loving support, and wonderful suggestions for this book. Also, my deep gratitude goes to Jill Kramer, Shannon Littrell, Amy Gingery, Anna Sachs, Ann Siwiak, Christine Holden, and—as always—to David for his patience, support, and love.

About the Author

Denise Linn is an internationally renowned teacher in the field of self-development. She is the author of the best-selling book *Sacred Space* and the award-winning *Feng Shui for the Soul*. Denise has written 14 books that are available in 24 languages, and has appeared in numerous documentaries and television shows worldwide. Denise gives seminars on six continents and is the founder of the International Institute of Soul Coaching®, which offers professional certification programs in life coaching.

For information about Denise's certification program and other lectures, visit her Website: **www.DeniseLinn.com**. Or write to her at:

Denise Linn Seminars
P.O. Box 759
Paso Robles, CA 93447

NOTES

NOTES

NOTES

NOTES

NOTES

NOTES

NOTES

NOTES

NOTES

NOTES

Hay House Titles of Related Interest

Being in Balance, by Dr. Wayne W. Dyer

Earth Wisdom: *A Heart-warming Mixture of the Spiritual, the Practical, and the Pro-active,* by Glennie Kindred

Everything I've Ever Done That Worked, by Lesley Garner

Goddesses: *Ancient Wisdom for Times of Change from Over 70 Goddesses,* by Sue Jennings, Ph.D.

Left to Tell: *Discovering God Amidst the Rwandan Holocaust,* by Immaculée Ilibagiza, with Steve Erwin

Lessons of a Lakota: *A Young Man's Journey to Happiness and Self-Understanding,* by Billy Mills, with Nicholas Sparks

Life's a Journey—Not a Sprint: *Navigating Life's Challenges and Finding Your Pathway to Success,* by Jennifer Lewis-Hall

Love Thyself: *The Message from Water III,* by Masaru Emoto

Mending the Past and Healing the Future with Soul Retrieval, by Alberto Villoldo, Ph.D.

Power Animals: *How to Connect with Your Animal Spirit Guide,* by Steven D. Farmer, Ph.D.

Secrets of the Lost Mode of Prayer: *The Hidden Power of Beauty, Blessing, Wisdom, and Hurt,* by Gregg Braden

Sylvia Browne's Lessons for Life, by Sylvia Browne

Trust Your Vibes: *Secret Tools for Six-Sensory Living,* by Sonia Choquette

Wisdom of the Heart: *Inspiration for a Life Worth Living,* by Alan Cohen

All of the above are available at your local bookstore,
or may be ordered through Hay House.

We hope you enjoyed this Hay House book.
If you'd like to receive a free catalog featuring additional
Hay House books and products, or if you'd like information
about the Hay Foundation, please contact:

Hay House, Inc.
P.O. Box 5100
Carlsbad, CA 92018-5100

(760) 431-7695 or (800) 654-5126
(760) 431-6948 (fax) or (800) 650-5115 (fax)
www.hayhouse.com® • www.hayfoundation.org

Published and distributed in Australia by: Hay House Australia Pty. Ltd. •
18/36 Ralph St. • Alexandria NSW 2015 • *Phone:* 612-9669-4299 •
Fax: 612-9669-4144 • www.hayhouse.com.au

Published and distributed in the United Kingdom by: Hay House UK, Ltd. •
292 B Kensal Rd., London W10 5BE • *Phone:* 44-20-8962-1230 •
Fax: 44-20-8962-1239 • www.hayhouse.co.uk

Published and distributed in the Republic of South Africa by: Hay House SA
(Pty), Ltd., P.O. Box 990, Witkoppen 2068 • *Phone/Fax:* 27-11-706-6612 •
orders@psdprom.co.za

Published in India by: Hay House Publications (India) Pvt. Ltd., 3 Hampton
Court, A-Wing, 123 Wodehouse Rd., Colaba, Mumbai 400005 • *Phone:* 91 (22)
22150557 or 22180533 • *Fax:* 91 (22) 22839619 • www.hayhouseindia.co.in

Distributed in India by: Media Star, 7 Vaswani Mansion, 120 Dinshaw
Vachha Rd., Churchgate, Mumbai 400020 • *Phone:* 91 (22) 22815538-39-40 •
Fax: 91 (22) 22839619 • booksdivision@mediastar.co.in

Distributed in Canada by: Raincoast • 9050 Shaughnessy St.,
Vancouver, B.C. V6P 6E5 • *Phone:* (604) 323-7100 • *Fax:* (604) 323-2600

Tune in to **HayHouseRadio.com®** for the best in inspirational
talk radio featuring top Hay House authors! And, sign up via the Hay House
USA Website to receive the Hay House online newsletter and stay informed
about what's going on with your favorite authors. You'll receive bimonthly
announcements about: Discounts and Offers, Special Events, Product
Highlights, Free Excerpts, Giveaways, and more!
www.hayhouse.com®